DOING THE TRUTH IN LOVE

Conversations about God,
Relationships, and Service

Michael J. Himes

DOING THE TRUTH IN LOVE

*Conversations about God,
Relationships, and Service*

MICHAEL J. HIMES

in collaboration with

Don McNeill, C.S.C., Andrea Smith Shappell, Jan Pilarski,
Stacy Hennessy, Katie Bergin, and Sarah Keyes

PAULIST PRESS
New York/Mahwah, N.J.

Excerpt from "As I Walked Out One Evening" from *W.H. Auden: Collected Poems* by W.H. Auden, copyright © 1949 and renewed 1968 by W. H. Auden. Reprinted by permission of Random House, Inc.

All the Scripture quotes in this volume are the author's own translations except where noted with the symbol NJB.

Those Scripture quotes noted with the symbol NJB are from *The New Jerusalem Bible* (Garden City, N.Y.: Doubleday & Company, Inc., 1985).

Copyright © 1995 by Michael J. Himes

All rights reserved. No part of this book may be reproduced or transmitted in any form or by any means, electronic or mechanical, including photocopying, recording, or by any information storage and retrieval system without permission in writing from the Publisher.

Library of Congress Cataloging-in-Publication Data

Himes, Michael J.
    Doing the truth in love : conversations about God, relationships, and service / Michael Himes : in collaboration with Don McNeill ... [et.al.]
        p. cm.
    Includes bibliographical references (p.)
    ISBN 0-8091-3584-1 (alk. paper)
    1. Service (Theology) 2. Love—Religious aspects—Christianity. 3. Church work—Catholic Church. 4. Vocation. 5. Catholic Church—Membership. I. McNeill, Donald P. II. Title.
BX2347.H55 1995
230'.2—dc20   95-8644
                                                                                  CIP

Published by Paulist Press
997 Macarthur Boulevard
Mahwah, New Jersey 07430

Printed and bound in the
United States of America

CONTENTS

Introduction   1

Chapter 1. Exploring the Mystery of God in Relationships   7

Chapter 2. Experiencing the Mystery of Not Being God   23
THE BLESSEDNESS OF LIMITS: RESPONSE BY JAN PILARSKI
Questions

Chapter 3. The Journey of Restlessness:
The Search for God   38
SHAKING THE GROUND BENEATH OUR FEET:
RESPONSE BY LOU NANNI
Questions

Chapter 4. Responding to God's Love:
Compassionate Service   50
RESPONSE BY MIKE BARKASY, SARAH KEYES,
BOB ELMER, KATIE BERGIN
Questions

Chapter 5. Vulnerability: Suffering the Mystery   68
BROKEN AND BLESSED: RESPONSE BY REG WEISSERT
Questions

Chapter 6. Conversing About the Mystery   83
THE SEARCH FOR UNDERSTANDING:
METHODS OF REFLECTING ON EXPERIENCE
RESPONSE BY DON MCNEILL, C.S.C., AND ANDREA SMITH SHAPPELL
Questions

Chapter 7. Sacramental Vision   100
WORD, SACRAMENT AND COMMUNITY:
RESPONSE BY RONALD WHITE
Questions

Chapter 8. Eucharist: Covenant, Thanksgiving and Destiny   118
EUCHARIST AS BEING FED BY THE POOR:
RESPONSE BY MARIA TERESA GASTON-WITCHGER
Questions

Chapter 9. Doing the Truth in Love   136

Contributors' Biographies   145

Resources for Continuing Conversations   150

THANKS—¡GRACIAS!

The most enjoyable part of working on this book was the process of conversing with many persons. We are particularly grateful to the students, in and out of the classroom, who raised questions which kept the discussions going as they reflected on the persons they encountered in Urban Plunges, Appalachian Programs, Summer Service Projects, etc. Supporting these service opportunities for students, we extend our gratitude to the staff of the Center for Social Concerns, the Institute for Church Life, the Alumni Association, and the ICL Advisory Council.

We thank Agnes McNeill Donohue, Margie Fink, Bob Hamma, Ingrid Schmidt, and Dominic Vachon for their thoughtful reading and suggestions for the evolving text.

We are grateful to the Notre Dame Department of Theology in which Michael taught for six years and to the residence hall communities in Keenan and Pasquerilla East, and to Rachel Tomás-Morgan and others who encouraged the writing of this book.

Typing and organizing transcriptions would have been impossible without the assistance of Anne McGuire, Ardis King, Sandy Barton, Carol Porter, Carol Grey, Margie Davis, Marty Tracy, Kristin Carlson, and Emy Lou Papandria. We appreciate the research of Margy Pfeil and Martin Connell. Sheryl Dyer, Linda Dunn, and Barbara Parker-Stephenson were the photographers who helped bring the words to life.

We thank Michael Barkasy, Bob Elmer, Katie Glynn, Lou Nanni, Regina Weissert, Ron White, and Maria Teresa Gaston-Witchger for their insightful responses which integrate theology with their life experience. Gracias to Fr. Theodore M. Hesburgh C.S.C., Dolores Lecke, Jim and Evelyn Whitehead, and Henri J. M. Nouwen for their book review and comments on the back cover. Those of us with spouses and families appreciate the words of encouragement and the space given so we could be creatively involved in this project.

We are grateful to Paulist Press and especially Richard Sparks for his encouragement and assistance throughout the process of developing the manuscript and the book. All involved with the Center for Social Concerns are deeply grateful to Michael Himes for the royalties from this book which will allow more students, alums, and others to "do the truth in love."

INTRODUCTION

COMPANIONS IN CONVERSATION: HIMES' PERSPECTIVE

Few needs are as pressing and as often go unmet in our world as the need for a place to converse. We all require somewhere, some circle of companions, where and with whom we can enter into the demanding task of trying to say what we experience and to understand what others say in response. There may be many places and opportunities for "passing the time of day," "shooting the breeze," "pleasant chat," although I suspect that for many such places and occasions are also becoming rare, but circles of conversation are precious, indeed. Such places may be libraries, for frequently the most valuable, far-ranging and transformative conversations are with people who are not present and do not happen to be living any longer. Thank God for books! If we did not have them, we would be forced to talk only to nearby contemporaries. Conversation, whether with those around us or those separated from us in space and time or, ideally, both, is necessary for thinking. How would we ever know what we do and feel and experience if we did not talk about our actions and feelings and experiences with others? This is true for everyone and it is certainly true for theologians.

While teaching at the University of Notre Dame, I was privileged to be part of several circles of conversation, one of the most fruitful of which was at the Center for Social Concerns, a particularly bright jewel in Notre Dame's crown. Thanks to the welcome and support of the Center's always gracious staff, I had many opportunities to talk with students, alumni and alumnae, and others engaged in discerning how the Christian call to service with one's neighbor can be lived out in a world where marriages are formed, children raised, mortgages paid and careers pursued. Through many conversations we talked about who God is, about relationships and what Christianity is about, and how we might reimagine our lives and our world in light of what we believe about God in the Christian tradition.

1

Don McNeill, C.S.C., Andrea Shappell and other members of the
Center's staff urged that some of these conversations be made available
to those not present there and then (again, thank God for books!). I was
initially reluctant, both because I doubted whether what I said in the
relaxed atmosphere of these conversations would be of interest to those
who had not been present and because of the difficulty in recalling
comments made on numerous occasions over the course of several years.
Ah, but the ever-resourceful folks at the Center had an answer for those
worries. They had been taping—and taping and taping and taping, and it
appeared that scarcely had an unrecorded word fallen from my lips. Don
McNeill suggested that a group of people go through these hours and
hours of audio and video-tape and select points to be transcribed which
they thought others might find helpful in thinking through their
experience of living Christianity. With extraordinary patience and
industry this was done. They also transcribed some audio tapes from a
few presentations given outside the Center for Social Concerns and from
some classroom sessions with students at Notre Dame. Of course, prose-
to-be-heard differs greatly from prose-to-be-read, and so I extensively
edited and rearranged the material.

At the urging of the group of colleagues who had selected the
material from the tapes, I have preserved the informal, conversational
tone of the originals. What we were not able to preserve, however, was
the context of the conversation, the back-and-forth exchange, the
questions or objections which led to clarifications and restatements. In
order to allow other voices than mine to be heard, seven chapters have a
comment, response or expansion from the experience of someone else
or a few persons. These are followed by questions by Stacy Hennessy to
prompt further personal or group conversation. It is my hope that the
book which has resulted carries some of the flavor of those conversation
circles which I so much appreciated at the Center for Social Concerns.

I suppose every writer has some imaginary reader in mind for a book. I
have had the great advantage of not having to imagine a reader—or, more
accurately, a hearer. For I recall with gratitude those who engaged in these
conversations with me from 1987 to 1993, and I think of the readers of this
book as being people like them. This is a book, therefore, for people who
do not want their religious life to be partitioned off from the rest of their
experience, men and women who will not allow water-tight bulkheads to
be erected between the deepest levels of their experience and questions
like how to choose a job, make a living, pay taxes, vote, and live with
neighbors. The reader may be young (like most of those who were part of
the original conversations) or not so young (like, alas, the writer). The
reader may be engaged full-time in service-work or exploring how the call

to love and service can be combined with supporting a family and pursuing a career. What the reader will be is someone who insists that what he or she believes makes a difference in fact, that theology not be an imposition on experience but an explication of it, that truth is not only what one believes but what one does. I have been gifted with such companions in conversation and am happy that other such readers join us.

COMPANIONS IN CONVERSATION: CENTER FOR SOCIAL CONCERNS PERSPECTIVE

The six of us, Don, Andrea, Jan, Stacy, Katie, and Sarah, engaged in the educational mission of the Center for Social Concerns at Notre Dame, have benefited from our ongoing conversation with Michael Himes since he joined the Department of Theology in the fall of 1987. As Michael mentions above, we began taping his responses to student questions emerging from their social concerns involvement. We also transcribed his presentations which led to conversations from a variety of contexts: continuing formation in ministry; religious education groups; human rights groups; homilies; responses to questions from parishes; preparation and "follow up" sessions for students in service learning experiences.

The Center encourages conversation which is interdisciplinary, cross-cultural, and intergenerational. We soon discovered that Himes' thoughts enabled and evoked conversations which were lively, animated, and transcended the usual communication barriers. We compiled his thoughts in such a way that we hope you and other readers will be drawn closer in thought and experience to God, others, and yourselves. We believe that his ideas lead to fresh discoveries of the mystery of God, Christ, and our participation in a restless search for truth.

The six of us who spent the weekend with Michael to finalize the book in April of 1994 tried to have all of you in mind. It was for this reason that we invited Regina Weissert, Michael Barkasy, Bob Elmer, Ron White, Lou Nanni, and Maria Teresa Gaston-Witchger to share responses from their personal experience to some of the chapters, in addition to our own. We hope their conversation with the insights of Michael will engage you to reflect your own personal story and faith journey.

We believe that your life experiences with joy and sorrow will bring you to each chapter with enthusiasm and passionate inquiry. We have come to this book from a variety of work and life situations, and thus we present a number of different starting points from which the importance of writing this book emerged.

- **Continuing education for life**—*Don McNeill, C.S.C., and Andrea Smith Shappell*

As educators whose primary role is one of facilitating small group discussion, we have seen many students who are raising deep questions about their faith find new insights and perspectives in discussion with Michael Himes. Our work at the Center for Social Concerns, our awareness of students' and alumni's restless desire to discover God in experiences of service and compassion, is very apparent in all facets of the Center's programs. Our hope is that this book allows students of all ages to reflect on the integration of faith and experience, whether they be persons raising children, grandparents, university students, or simply anyone who is open to exploring dimensions of faith.

- **Pastoral, campus, and social ministries**—*Jan Pilarski and Stacy Hennessy*

In our experiences in one or more of the ministries of campus minister, community organizer, theologian, and diocesan social ministry coordinator, we found Michael Himes' insights into God's self-revelation refreshing for the variety of persons with whom we work. The insights on issues such as service, experience, and sacrament help us all to reflect more deeply on life's journey, and to appreciate how much there is to gain by sharing with each other our questions, experiences, and challenges. Through these discussions we are led to deeper relationships with one another and, in doing so, come closer and closer to God.

- **Students and young adults in service**—*Katie Bergin and Sarah Keyes*

Participating in this book has really been a blessing. To be engaged with others in a conversation about love, God, truth, and service—topics many of us probably do not openly talk about enough —is a gift. We just graduated from Notre Dame and are entering service experiences in the Holy Cross Associates, Sarah domestically, and Katie in Chile. The ideas and content of this book as well as the wonderful people connected with it continue to shape our thinking as we enter our time of service and our open future. We are excited by the hope that this book will expose those who are burning with questions, those whose experiences have left them confused and searching, to deeper insights that lead to further action for a more just and humane world.

From this variety of starting points we now invite Michael Himes to present an overview of the book and its challenge for our conversations about doing the truth in love.

THE INVITATION TO RISK CONTINUING
THE CONVERSATION

Any conversation requires taking risks. The greatest risk is that of being changed by what one hears the conversation partner say and, perhaps even more, by what one hears oneself say. Another risk is that the conversation may go nowhere. You have every right to demand that you have some notice in advance that these conversations go somewhere. And, ever careful as I am of the reader's rights, I will tell you what we shall be talking about.

No word is more central to theology than "God," and yet I doubt that there is any word more often misunderstood by Christians. We begin by trying to clarify what we mean by that all-important, much misused word, and I suggest in chapter 1 that it is least wrongly understood as the name of a very particular relationship. Having spoken about God, we turn to us, that is, to God's creatures, and in chapter 2 I maintain that the most fundamental of all religious statements is that I am not God and that this is a good thing. Chapter 3 then takes up what I firmly believe to be the truest statement ever made about human beings, that we are all dissatisfied, and asks how we can live with our restlessness.

Chapter 4 follows from what we say about God and about human beings as "the image of God" and so asks the question which the first hearers of the gospel asked: "What then must we do?" (Acts 2:37) And the answer, I suggest, is that we must do what God is. But we cannot pretend that any of this is immediately obvious in a world marked by suffering, pain, and death. No one has the right to talk about the deepest issues of human experience and brush lightly by the mystery of evil, and so we must face that mystery in chapter 5.

The next chapter asks a question which will certainly have occurred to you, intelligent and perceptive reader that you are, by that point if not long before: Why are you bothering to read this book at all? That question may take heightened form if you have agreed with me through the earlier chapters that Christianity is first of all about *doing* the truth. Why then are we *thinking* and *talking* about it instead? Chapter 6 addresses the point of theology and its enrichment by ordinary experience.

Chapter 7 brings us a key contribution of the Catholic theological tradition, sacramentality. But we shall not be talking about the seven great ritual celebrations which we designate by the term "sacraments." I shall suggest that sacramentality is a way—a very specifically Catholic way—of seeing the whole world and everyone and everything in it. Chapter 8 turns attention to the eucharist as the revelation of who we are and what we are meant for. In a sense, it restates everything we will have said to that point and validates it through the eucharist. And finally chapter 9 asks us to reflect on what (I hope) the whole conversation has been doing: expanding our imagination.

Now, I have every hope that this description of where we will go and what we will be talking about is sufficiently cryptic that you are wondering, "Whatever is Himes going on about?" And that is an excellent starting point for any conversation.

1
EXPLORING THE MYSTERY
OF GOD IN RELATIONSHIPS

Ubi caritas et amor, Deus ibi est.

Wherever there is charity and love, there is God.

I. UNDERSTANDING GOD AS MYSTERY

The mystery of God is an enormous topic. First of all, let us center on the word "mystery." This word is often used when we speak of God, but we have not perhaps taken it seriously enough. When we speak of God as the "ultimate" or "deepest" or "richest" or "most profound mystery," what do we mean? What does it mean to say that God is a mystery?

There are two meanings to the word "mystery." One is the way in which we use the term when we talk about an Agatha Christie mystery, a murder mystery, where the problem is that there are missing clues. If we could only get our hands on the missing pieces and organize them in the right way, we would see the solution. We would know that the butler did it, and the mystery would be solved.

But that is not what we mean when we talk about God as a mystery. Then we are using "mystery" in a quite different sense—in what I refer to as the Caterpillar sense of mystery. Think of one of the truly profound books of the nineteenth century, Lewis Carroll's *Alice in Wonderland*. Do you remember the passage in which Alice, who is very small at that point in the story, encounters the Caterpillar seated on a mushroom smoking a waterpipe? The conversation begins with the Caterpillar asking Alice the question, "Who are *you*?" Alice replies that, because of all the strange transformations which she has passed through so far that day, she is no longer sure who she is. "Explain yourself!" the Caterpillar demands. "I can't explain *myself*, I'm afraid, Sir," said Alice, "because I am not myself, you see." The Caterpillar replies that he does not see, and Alice tries to explain that the extraordinary things that have happened to her, especially her shifts in size, have left her confused. She says that she is sure that the Caterpillar would feel the same had such things happened to him. The Caterpillar insists that he would not fail to know who he is, and when Alice responds that it all feels very strange "to *me*," he returns to his original question: "You!" said the Caterpillar contemptuously. "Who are *you*?"

The Caterpillar's question is, in fact, the rigorously logical question to ask, because every one of Alice's questions or replies returns to the pronoun "I." And the Caterpillar, who like everyone in Wonderland is a rigorous logician, insists that Alice define her terms. Before he can answer her questions, she has to explain who this "I" is to whom she keeps referring. Alice's frustration in the conversation comes from the fact that there is no answer to the Caterpillar's question. I grant you, if you stop at a gas station to ask for directions, you don't expect metaphysical argument, and so one can understand Alice's frustration. But the Caterpillar's question is not an idle one. It is a very important question, indeed: "Who are *you*?" The difficulty is that none of us has a good answer. Notice: we are not asked for a description. Don't answer with a name, because we English speakers know on excellent authority that "a rose by any other name would smell as sweet." Don't answer by telling where you live, or what your work is, or where you went to school, or who your parents are. Don't answer with your age or your social security number. All of that is description. And the Caterpillar's question does not ask for a description but for a definition.

"Who are *you*?" The problem is that we don't know. It is a question without an answer. It is mystery in a very rich sense, the sense in which all of us are mysteries to ourselves. One of the greatest theological minds the Christian tradition has yet seen, St. Augustine, wrote his *Confessions* in part as an exploration of the mystery, "Who is Augustine?" He knew that he could not answer the question because the moment he did, he became more than he had said in his answer and so made the answer false. If I could tell you in one wonderful, flashing, brilliantly insightful statement that this is who I am, the very act of making the statement makes me more than who I was, and so the answer is no longer right. The very attempt to answer the question pushes me past any answer I can give to the question.

That is what we mean when we talk about God as mystery. We are talking about something so closely interwoven into who we are that it becomes impossible to answer. God is mystery not because God is so distant but because God is so terribly close; understanding who God is is so tied up with understanding who I am and why I am that the question "Who is God?" becomes as impossible to answer as the question "Who am I?"

It is of great importance that we recognize this, for it requires us constantly to attempt to purify our consciousness of God, to remind ourselves that in talking about God we are talking about absolute mystery. Blasphemy is always the danger in preaching, in theology, in catechesis, because we can so easily begin to identify our best images of God with *God*.

The story is told of a distinguished theologian that, when addressing new students for the first time, he would enter the lecture hall, proceed to the podium, and begin by saying, "God." Then he would pause dramatically during the hush while the students waited to find out what he had to say about God. He would then tell the students, "Whatever came into your head when I said the word 'God,' is not God." And that is exactly correct. The first and most important thing to know in theology is that whatever you think of when you hear the word "God" is not God. However deep, however rich, however noble, however powerful, however loving, however scripturally-based or traditionally-sanctioned, whatever the image is, it is not God because God remains mystery. We must take that very seriously.

And so we need to recognize that the word "God" is not a proper name. It is not the name of some great big person somewhere "out there." The word "God" functions like *x* in algebra. It is the stand-in for the mystery, just as, when someone works out an algebraic equation, all the attention focuses on *x* which designates that which is unknown. So, too, the word "God" functions as a handy bit of shorthand for the absolute mystery which grounds and supports all that exists. Now, I grant you that it becomes awkward to talk about "the absolute mystery that grounds and supports all that exists," so we just say "God." One could just as well call it "Charlie" or "Mary Ann," but traditionally we have used "God." The word is a stand-in for absolute mystery.

But, acknowledging that there is no final and fully correct way of imaging or speaking about God, is there any way less hopelessly inadequate than every other way? The great western religious traditions have at their cores claims about how one might least wrongly think and speak about God. And so, of course, has Christianity.

II. UNDERSTANDING GOD AS *AGAPE*

What the Christian tradition maintains is the least inadequate expression for God finds its clearest, sharpest, simplest statement in one of the last-written documents of the collection of early Christian documents which we call the New Testament, the first letter of John.

There we read that "God is love" (1 Jn 4:8 and 16). But the love which is offered as the least wrong way to think and speak about God is of a very peculiar sort: *agape*. *Agape* is a Greek word meaning love which is purely other-directed, love which seeks no return, love which does not want anything back. Perhaps, so as not to confuse it with the many other meanings which we attach to the word "love" in English, we might translate *agape* as "pure self-gift."

One of the most astonishing statements in the New Testament is found in the section of Matthew's gospel which we call the sermon on the mount (Mt 5–7). In some ways we could say that it functions as a kind of constitution for the kingdom of God. The very fact that Jesus' sermon takes place on a mountain recalls Moses coming down the mountain to proclaim the laws of God. And as Moses began his address to Israel with a kind of summary statement of what followed—we call the summary the ten commandments—so Jesus begins with a summary, the beatitudes.

The middle of the sermon consists of a number of comparisons between the Mosaic law and the new law of the kingdom, in which Jesus keeps "upping the ante" on the statements with which his hearers would have been so familiar: "You have heard it said to you that...but I say to you..." (Mt 5:21–47). You have heard it said that you shall not kill, but I tell you that you must not act or speak in anger. You have heard it said that you shall not commit adultery, but I tell you that you must not think lustfully. You have heard it said that you must not divorce except under certain circumstances, but I tell you that divorce is never permissible. You have heard it said that you must not swear falsely, but I tell you that you must not swear at all. These comparisons climax with "You have heard it said that you shall love your neighbor and hate your enemy. But I tell you that you must love your enemies and pray for those who persecute you" (Mt 5:43–44).

This has been made even more startlingly concrete in the preceding verses: "If someone slaps you on the right cheek, offer him the other cheek as well. If someone wants to take you to law to get your coat, give him your shirt as well. If someone demands that you go one mile, go two miles with him." But, one might well ask, on what possible grounds should we act in such an unheard-of fashion? After all, what if the person has slapped us unjustly? What if he or she has no right to my coat, let alone my shirt? What if he or she has no basis for expecting me to go a single mile, no less two? It is here that Matthew's gospel offers its astounding claim. Perhaps, as with so many other statements of the New Testament, we have heard it so often that it no longer shocks us. But it should, for in answer to the obvious question, "Why should we act in such a strange and unaccountable way?" Jesus responds that we must do so in order to "be children of your Father in heaven who makes the sun shine on the wicked as well as the good and sends rain to fall on the just as well as the unjust" (Mt 5:45).

This is an absolutely shocking claim. We wouldn't get away with saying this sort of thing in most pulpits today, let me tell you. Why should we act in the peculiar fashion which Jesus has described? Because we are God's children and ought to act like our parent. And that parent makes the sun shine on the good and the wicked, makes the rain fall on the just and the unjust. Please notice that what Jesus maintains is that our Father in heaven finds ethics very dull. Our Father in heaven finds moral theology a bit of a yawn. Our Father in heaven doesn't especially care whether you are good or wicked or whether you are just or unjust. Your Father in heaven simply loves you. There are no bounds to God's love, so do not put any bounds to yours. "Be perfect as your heavenly Father is perfect" (Mt 5:48). You may not love your Father in heaven, but your Father in heaven still loves you. So you be perfect as your heavenly Father is perfect: love those who hate you; do good to those who persecute you.

Let's explore this amazing claim a bit. It lies at the root of the whole Christian way of understanding what we mean by "God" and therefore also of understanding what it is to be a human being. It is said again and again in the parables of Jesus. Many of the parables are problematic to us, which is why we often tend to water them down when we preach or talk about them. Take, for example, the prodigal son (Lk 15:11–32), a parable which we have frequently distorted. Often we turn it into a story about repentance, when in fact the parable is at pains to exclude any element of repentance. Approach the story fresh, as though you have never heard it before. And keep in mind two points, both of which are necessary in order to understand the relationship of the three main figures in the story, the father and his two sons. First, remember how patriarchal the organization of ancient near eastern society was. One's social, economic, even religious standing depended on one's relation to the head of the household. Second, recall that in Jesus' time, inheritance was governed by primogeniture, i.e. all property went to the eldest son; daughters and younger sons inherited nothing.

And so the story begins: once there was a man who had two sons. The younger one came to him and said, "Dad, why should I hang around until you finally die? Give me my share of the inheritance now." The opening of the story should shock the hearer right off the bat. How could any son say such a thing to his father? We find it reprehensible, and we are by no means as respectful of parents as was the society in which Jesus taught and in which the author of Luke's gospel wrote. Note, too, that whether the father is alive or dead, this impertinent son inherits nothing. The whole estate should go to his older brother. The younger boy has no share. His demand is not only cruel in its form but nonsensical in its import. So what should the response of a respectable, upright, just, and God-fearing father have been? Probably a good slap. Presumably Jesus' hearers would have agreed that the proper response for the father in the story would be to tell the disrespectful twerp to mind his manners. But instead what we hear is that the father divided up the estate, turned half of it into cash and gave it to the younger son. So, at the outset of the parable, we know two things: the younger son is thoughtless and self-centered, and the father is a hopelessly irresponsible parent. This is not a story about good parenting techniques.

The younger son went off to a far country and wasted his money on wine, women and song. Then a great famine descended on the land where he was living and he was reduced to tending pigs. He was so hungry that he envied the slop thrown to the pigs. That detail is a wonderful touch. It is, after all, a Jewish story. The son has ended up envying non-kosher animals, a graphic ancient Jewish equivalent to having hit the bottom of the barrel. Eventually the younger son came to his senses and said to himself, "At home, even the servants eat better than I am. I know what I will do. I will go home to my father and say, 'Father, I have sinned before heaven and against you. I am not worthy to be called your son. Treat me as one of your hired hands'" (Lk 15:17–19). And he set off for home.

Please notice: only one motive is given in the story for the son's return home—he can eat better there. There is not a syllable of regret for how badly he has treated his father or for the fact that he is alienated from his family. The sole motive is that he is hungry and can get a good meal at home. Indeed, to underscore the point, the story has the younger son concoct a prepared statement. He puts together his little speech to tug at the father's heartstrings and heads home.

The father saw him coming from a great distance and ran out to meet him. And as we might anticipate from this irresponsible parent, the father does not ask the obvious questions: "Where have you been? What have you been doing? Why are you dressed so badly? What happened to all the money I gave you?" Nor does he wait to discover if the son has learned his lesson. When the son launches into his prepared text, "Father, I have sinned before heaven and against you," etc., and before he even reaches the last line, "Treat me as one of your hired hands," the father turns to the servants and commands that they get a ring for the son's finger, sandals for his feet, and a robe to put on him, and that they slay the fatted calf for the welcoming feast. And so the father scoops the son up, takes him into the house, and the party begins.

Where are we at this point in the story? This is the last time we see the younger son in the story, and so far as we know, he has not changed in the least from what he was at the outset. He was a selfish egoist at the beginning and he's a selfish egoist to the end. There has been no conversion, no repentance. We also know that the father is a hopelessly irresponsible parent. Indeed, we might well wonder if the reason the son is impossible is that the father is so inept.

And now enters the much injured older brother. After working all day in the fields (I must admit that the story lays it on a bit thick here), this faithful and hard-working son comes home to discover a party in progress. He asks one of the servants what is going on and, when he learns that it is a welcome-home party for his wastrel younger brother, refuses to go in to dinner. At this point, the older son should have had our sympathies, since he has been clearly the wronged party. But to refuse to break bread with his father, no matter who else is at the table! In our far less family-oriented world, we would find it a bit much for a child to refuse to eat with his or her parents because of a fight with a brother or sister who is at the table. In the ancient near east, such behavior would have been unpardonable. And once again, the father responds in precisely the way we have come to expect: he comes out to plead with him. And now we hear the wonderful final conversation which is what the whole story has been leading up to.

Remember, in Luke's gospel Jesus tells this story to the scribes and Pharisees who have been complaining that he welcomes sinners and is even willing to sit down at table with them (Lk 15:1–3). Hear the conversation between the father and his older son which concludes the parable in terms of that unsympathetic audience to whom the story was first told. The older son complains to the father, "I have worked and slaved for you constantly and you have given me nothing, not so much as a kid goat to have a party with my friends. But when this wastrel comes home, you throw this big party for him. It's wrong! It's unjust!" And the father's response is, "Son, everything that I have is yours"—which may be true, save that there is fifty percent less, thanks to the younger son; we should not lose sight of the fact that the older son really has been wronged. "Everything I have is yours," the father continues, "but the one who was lost is found. The one who was dead is alive. We had to rejoice." End of story.

Clearly, this is not a story about repentance. What is it about? I suggest to you that it is about the incomprehensibility of the love and mystery of God. The climax of the story is that final conversation. The older son's argument is that the father's behavior is absurd and, what is more, unjust. And note that the father does not dispute the justice of the older son's complaints; he simply regards them as irrelevant. For the father isn't concerned with justice. The father is concerned with *agape*, absolute unconditional self-gift. The older son can argue, "Look, he demanded money he had no right to and he lost it. He has never shown the least regard for you or for this family. He doesn't deserve the party which you are giving him. This is unjust." And, given the older son's perspective, he is quite right. The father can reply, "But the young man was lost; now he's found. He was dead; now he's alive." What is the obvious response? Have a party. And the father is right, given the father's perspective.

The parable's point is to underscore that there are two different perspectives, each understandable in itself and each incomprehensible to the other. God does not see as human beings see, as the gospel reminds us again and again. If you find yourself saying, "I simply don't understand how God can act that way," then you may very well have gotten the point of the parable. Presumably the scribes and the Pharisees who first heard the story could not figure it out either. If you start with the conviction that our primary relationship to God is one of justice, then, Jesus seems to insist, you will certainly misunderstand God.

Perhaps the reason the Pharisees are given so much attention in the synoptic gospels is not only their historical importance but because the writers recognized that Pharisaism is a possibility for Christians. The problem with the Pharisees as they are depicted in the New Testament is that they think they know who and what God is and how God acts. God is the law-giver, and God's concern is that the law be observed, and, therefore, not to keep the law is *ipso facto* to put oneself outside the love of God. Imagine how they had to respond to an itinerant rabbi from Galilee who told them shocking parables in which he claimed their relationship with God was not one of justice or of keeping laws. For, as the parable we have been considering maintains, the younger son doesn't deserve anything, but God loves him in any event. After all, what is it to you if God is generous? Tax collectors and prostitutes are wicked and unjust, but God makes the sun shine on the good and the wicked and the rain fall on the just and the unjust. Your concern should simply be to be perfect as your heavenly Father is perfect. No wonder such a message drove the Pharisees crazy. We had to be cautioned about Pharisaism precisely because it would always remain an option for us as Christian believers. When they actually hear it, the gospel drives a lot of Christians crazy, too.

Of course, the question of punishment, i.e. of hell and damnation, will arise in many people's minds, and quite rightly. But damnation does not mean that God ceases to love the one damned. If that were true, then the sinner would be more powerful than God, since the sinner would have the power to make God, who is love, *agape*, something less than God. No, God's love is constant, unchanging and perfect. Damnation means that the sinner refuses finally and absolutely to accept being loved and to love in response. The damned may not love God, but God continues to love the damned. After all, the love of God is what holds us in existence. If God does not love you, you're not damned. You simply aren't. What supports our existence and holds us in being is God's love. We exist by the fact that God gives God's self to us at every moment. Therefore, of course, God loves the damned. God loves everything that exists just because it exists. Indeed, that is what makes it exist: God loves it into being.

Let me give you an image which comes from Gregory of Nyssa at the end of the fourth century. The difference between heaven and hell is described in this story he tells: Picture yourself walking out on a bright sunny day with healthy eyes. You will experience the sunlight as something wonderful and pleasant and beneficent. Now, picture yourself walking out on exactly the same bright sunny day, but with a diseased eye. You will now experience the sunlight as something terrible and painful and awful, something to shy away from. Well, the sun didn't change. You did.

That is the point about heaven and hell. Heaven and hell are exactly the same thing: the love of God. If you have always wanted the love of God, congratulations, you got heaven. If you don't want the love of God, too bad, you are stuck for all eternity. God remains God. God makes the sun shine on the just and the unjust, the rain fall on the good and the wicked. If you don't want rain or sun, too bad, you are still going to get them. The question is not that God changes in response to us. It is that we are judged by our response to the absoluteness of God's self gift.

If, then, you are willing to accept that the Christian tradition holds that the least wrong way to think and speak about the absolute mystery which is God is as pure and perfect self-gift, *agape*, you can begin to perceive the richest and deepest insight of the Christian tradition into the doctrine of God. It is a doctrine which we have managed in the course of nineteen centuries to dilute almost to the point of irrelevance. Please notice that the Christian tradition holds that God is *agape*, i.e. love in the sense of self-gift, *not* that God is a lover. The tradition, e.g. 1 John 4:8 and 16, says that God is *love*, not that God is *one who loves*. "Love" is not the name of a person. "Love" is the name of a relationship between persons. That, I suggest to you, is the single richest insight into the mystery of God that the Christian tradition has to offer.

III. UNDERSTANDING GOD AS RELATIONSHIP

This seems to imply that we should first think of God not as a person but as a relationship between persons. "Now," you may say to yourself, "what a weird, silly statement! Who in heaven's name has ever thought of God like that?" Well, you have—at least, you have if you meant what you said when you professed the Nicene Creed or, even more commonly, when you began your prayer "in the name of the Father and of the Son and of the Holy Spirit." When we say those words, are we not claiming that God is a person but is the relationship between three? That is the whole point of the doctrine of the Trinity, is it not? The word "God" is the name of a kind of communal relationship. God is not the one, God is the relatedness of the three. This idea is precisely what lies at the heart of the great Christian claim about the meaning of the word "God," that the least hopelessly wrong way of understanding God is to think of God as a relationship even before thinking of God as a person.

Now, of course, there is a problem with this. When was the last time you heard a decent homily or conversation on the Trinity? In practice, most of our fellow believers do not find that the doctrine of the Trinity makes any difference to the concrete understanding of their lives: how they pray, how they live out their marriages, how they bring up their children, why they are part of the church, how they relate to their neighbors, how they spend their money, or how they vote. The doctrine of the Trinity seems simply irrelevant to these concerns.

The great American philosopher, William James, held that if something is true, it makes a difference, and if it makes no difference, it is not true. The great problem with the doctrine of the Trinity is that for most people it makes no difference. Most people understand it as very strange information about God, but of no particular importance to them. I have often remarked that, if this Sunday all the clergy stood up in their pulpits and told the parishioners, "We have a letter from the pope announcing that God is not three, but four," most people would simply groan, "Oh, will these changes never stop?" But aside from having to figure out how to fit the fourth one in when making the sign of the cross, the news would make no difference to anyone because it has become concretely irrelevant to people.

And yet the Trinity is not just one doctrine among others in the creed, it is the central Christian doctrine. If this is so, then what a shocking thing that it makes no difference. Notice the way in which the creed has traditionally been organized. We do not actually say that we believe in the Trinity. Rather, the whole creed is a trinitarian statement. "We believe in God the Father who...," followed by the doctrines of creation and providence. "And in God the Son who...," followed by the doctrines of the incarnation, redemption, and resurrection. "And in God the Spirit who...," followed by statements of belief in scripture, the church, sacraments, and eschatology. The Trinity is not one doctrine among others; it is the shape of all doctrine. The whole profession of the Christian faith is a profession of faith in the Trinity.

Our usual language for talking about the Trinity sometimes is not very helpful. The language of "Father," "Son," and "Spirit" is scripturally based, to be sure (Mt 28:19), but it is not the only language which has been used in the course of the church's tradition. For example, St. Augustine suggested a number of alternative ways of thinking and speaking about the Trinity, one of which was "Lover," "Beloved," and the "Love" between them. I think that this language penetrates deeply into what the tradition is really expressing in the doctrine of the Trinity. What is meant by the word "God" is an eternal outpouring of self, a continual giving which is accepted and returned in continual giving, and the Spirit, that which unites the Lover and the Beloved, is agape. And so, I suggest to you that we must recapture an understanding of God as the ultimate mystery, least wrongly approached as the relationship of perfect self-gift.

We have all heard statements in scripture which provide insight into that claim. For example, we have all heard a thousand times: "Wherever two or three are gathered in my name, there am I in their midst" (Mt 18:20). We tend to reduce that statement too easily to "I shall be with you in spirit," with a small "s" on spirit. It is the kind of thing we say when apologizing for not being able to accept an invitation or attend an event. But let us take Jesus' words seriously. Might it not then mean, "Where two or three come together in genuine agape, true mutual self-gift, there I am"?

At the eucharist of the Lord's supper on Holy Thursday, during the re-enactment of the washing of the disciples' feet, the traditional text which the church has sung for centuries is, *Ubi caritas et amor, Deus ibi est*, "Wherever there is charity and love, there is God." Take that seriously! If God is least wrongly thought of as *agape*, then wherever you see charity and love, there's God. If the word "God" is least wrongly understood as a particular kind of relationship, then wherever you see that relationship genuinely lived out, wherever you see charity and love, you see the presence of God.

In John's gospel, immediately after Jesus washes his disciples' feet at the start of the last supper (Jn 13:2–16), he says to them: "I give you one new commandment: love one another. You must love one another as I have loved you. By your love for one another all will know that you are my disciples" (Jn 13:34-35). The whole last supper discourse in John's gospel (chapters 13-17) is a magnificent reflection on love and communion. And, astonishingly, not once does Jesus ever tell his disciples to love God, although we are repeatedly told to love one another. For God is not the object of love; in a sense, God is not even the subject of love. God is simply the love. What happens when you serve your brother or sister is that you are enacting the meaning of the word "God." One could say that "God" is closer to being a verb than a noun. "God" is what is done, not the one who does it, nor the one to whom it is done. God is the doing, the loving. That extraordinary metaphor in 1 John 4:8 and 16, "God is *agape*," self-giving love, is what lies at the heart of the doctrine of the Trinity.

For, you see, we Christians do not believe in a "supreme being" out there someplace who creates the universe and whom we are supposed to love in return. That is not what Christianity is about at all. We do not claim that there is a being "out there." We maintain that if you want to know what we mean by "God," you start with the agapic love which is shed abroad in our hearts here. The notion of a supreme being belittles God. Calling someone or something the supreme being presumes that there is a class of things, beings, and that one of those beings is the number one being in the class, the supreme one. But that is, of course, precisely what Christianity denies about God: God is not a member of any class. God is not one being among many beings, not even the supreme one. St. Thomas Aquinas taught that God is the power of being, being itself (*esse*), but not a being (*ens*), supreme or otherwise. Thomas made "God" more like a verb than a noun. And so did the first letter of John, in that case, the verb being "love."

Where, then, does the doctrine of God lead us? It leads us to community. For obviously we cannot talk about God meaningfully in the Christian tradition unless in some way we attempt to live in a community where genuine *agape* is realized. Only by participating in self-gift can one come to know what we are trying to designate by the word "God." If you want to know who God is, give yourself away.

To explore this idea further, think of another familiar parable told in Luke's gospel, the story of the good Samaritan (Lk 10:29-37). Recall that the parable is attached to the discussion of the two great commandments (Lk 10:25-28). A scribe, i.e. someone learned in the Mosaic law, wants to show Jesus up as lacking the credentials to be a rabbi. So he asks Jesus what is necessary for eternal life. Jesus responds by asking what the scribe has read in the scriptures. The scribe answers, "Love God with all your heart and all your soul and all your strength and all your mind, and love your neighbor as yourself." And Jesus assents,

"Right, do that and you will have life." But the scribe, not wanting to let Jesus off the hook, persists by asking, "And who is my neighbor?" This then leads Jesus to tell the parable. Please note: the parable is a clarification of the conversation about the two great commandments, and what it says about those two commandments is very striking, indeed.

A certain man on his way down from Jerusalem to Jericho was set upon by robbers who beat him and left him for dead on the side of the road. A priest came along, saw the man lying there bloodied, crossed to the other side of the road and passed by. A Levite, i.e. an official in the temple, a sort of sacristan, also came along, saw the wounded man, crossed to the opposite side of the road and continued on. Then a Samaritan, i.e. a half-breed Jew at odds with other Jews both racially and religiously, came along the road and was moved with compassion when he saw the wounded man. So he stopped to help him, brought him to an inn, and paid for the care of the injured man. "Now," Jesus asks the scribe, "who do you think was the neighbor to the man who was attacked by the robbers?" Of course, the scribe replies that the neighbor is the one who helped him, and he is told by Jesus to go and act in the same way.

What is the parable about? Clearly, its primary point is that everyone is the neighbor, including those who are separated by racial, ethnic, and religious differences. But if that is the sole point, then why, in a story so lacking in details, bother to mention that the first two passers-by were a priest and a Levite? If the only point to be made is that everyone is called upon to be neighbor to everyone else, all that is needed in the story is two Jews. Why a priest and a Levite? Also, why include the detail that the priest and Levite not only passed the wounded man by, but did so by crossing over to the other side of the road? On the road between Jerusalem and Jericho, where would one expect a priest and a Levite to be going or coming from? The temple. And what would they do in the temple? Offer worship to God. And why do they not assist the wounded man? Because he is bloodied, and touching anything bloody would render them unclean, non-kosher, and so incapable of participation in the rites in the temple. That is why they carefully cross on the other side— so that no blood will touch them. But the Samaritan does not worship in the temple; he does not care about the question of ritual impurity. And so he stops to help the injured man. Undoubtedly, the story is about how marvelous it is that an enemy, a Samaritan, would help a Jew—that being neighbor knows no boundaries.

But there is another element which we ought not miss in the parable. After all, remember that it flows from a discussion of the two great commandments, to love God with one's whole being and to love one's neighbor. And the story makes the point that anyone who thinks that loving your neighbor might interfere with loving God simply does not know what loving God means. One can only love God with one's whole heart, soul, strength and mind if one also loves the neighbor. That is what the priest and the Levite missed. They were so concerned about worshiping God that they could not help a neighbor lest it get in the way of their worship. Jesus' point to the scribe is that anything which prevents you from helping your neighbor is certainly not the worship or love of God.

How can one square that with one's religious duties if one is a Pharisee? If you are worried about Jesus and his disciples not washing their hands before lunch (Lk 11:38 and Mt 15:1–2), how can you possibly deal with this parable? It seems designed to raise the eyebrows of precisely good, solid, religiously inclined people. But we must not forget that it was the good, solid, religiously inclined who decided that the sort of person who went about telling such parables had to be killed.

This is why, ultimately, orthopraxis always precedes orthodoxy. Before our tradition was called "Christianity," it was simply referred to as "the Way" (Acts 9:2). First of all, it is a way of life. One has to *do* the doctrine before one can understand the doctrine. One does not know and then do. After all, if you had to understand the doctrine and mystery of the eucharist correctly before you celebrated and participated in it, which one of us would ever have received our first communions? Long before I was taught religion lessons, I was taught to pray. And that is just as it should be. Practice precedes doctrine.

So, we maintain that in the person of Jesus of Nazareth we have the embodiment of what we mean by the word "God." Jesus is God in human terms, so if you want to know what we mean by the word "God," look at Jesus of Nazareth. Although we recognize many modes of Jesus' continuing presence with us, we have frequently talked about the eucharist as the "real presence." In the eucharist we find Jesus of Nazareth, and in Jesus we find God incarnate. But consider the eucharist. It is something that is eaten so that people have life, something that is drunk so that people are refreshed. What a profound symbolic act revealing the great Christian insight: if you seek to know who God is, look at Jesus of Nazareth; if you seek to know who Jesus is, he is the one who is eaten so that we may be nourished. The eucharist is the great acting-out of who Jesus, the self-revelation of God in human terms, is: the one who gives himself away fully and without reserve. So if you wish to find God, give yourself away. When we celebrate the eucharist, we enact what we mean by the word "God."

The fundamental Christian insight is that God is *agape*, that of all of the possible ways to think about God, no one of which is sufficient in and of itself, the least inadequate one is to think of God as pure and perfect self-gift, as the relationship of agapic love, and so as an action of service for the good of the other. We are called to participate in the very acting out of the life of God. That is what we mean when we say that the Spirit of God dwells in us. We are familiar with the image of Christians as "temples of the Holy Spirit." This is a rich image in many ways, but it can be misleading if it is heard statically, i.e. as a statement that the Spirit resides in us. Rather, the Spirit moves through us; the Spirit is within us to lead us to act. The Spirit does not dwell in us as in a box or a container. The Spirit energizes, the Spirit is what activates. Ultimately, the Spirit leads us to act out the meaning of the word "God."

But talking about "God" as the ultimate mystery obviously implies that I am not God. And if there is God and I am not God, then in some way I am dependent upon that ultimate mystery—or, in the terms of the Jewish and Christian traditions, I am a creature. And that is the not especially comfortable notion to which we must now turn in Chapter 2.

Questions

1. Explain how God can be more accurately thought of as a verb rather than as a noun.

2. If God is not some "supreme being out there," then what or who is God? How do we comunicate with God? Describe our relationship with God.

3. How have you previously understood the Trinity? How do you understand it now?

4. If God equally loves the just and the unjust, then how should we understand the rewards and punishments of saints and sinners? What does this understanding of God as lover of all do to our understanding of salvation?

Journal Questions

5. Describe God in your journal as though you were describing God to your best friend.

6. Reflect on the times in your life when you have felt most loved by

God by a) loving others and b) being loved. Tell each story in some detail and describe what it is you learned about God through these experiences.

7. Reflect on how it is sometimes difficult to love our enemies. Write about one person whom you find difficult to love. Why is it difficult? How can the God who is *agape* assist us in loving in a purely selfless way?

8. Write a parable in which you illustrate the limitless love of God.

2
EXPERIENCING THE MYSTERY OF NOT BEING GOD

The mass of men lead lives of quiet desperation.
–Henry David Thoreau

His state was divine, yet he did not cling to his equality
with God but emptied himself to assume the condition of a servant,
becoming human as all other human beings.
–Philippians 2:6–7

Consider what is, from the perspective of the Christian tradition, the deepest and most basic fact about us: we are creatures. What does being a creature mean? Certainly, it is a deeply important, perhaps shattering statement to say that the foundation of one's own existence is not in one's self, that the purpose and meaning of one's life are not determined by one's self, that our being and our meaning are given to us. If you can say that without being frightened, it is a fair bet that you don't understand what you've said.

I. THE GOODNESS OF BEING CREATURE

No one is ever completely secure. I am not a person of very adventurous disposition. I think that trying a new toothpaste is one of life's great explorations. I like to know what I'm going to be doing two years from Thursday. I am the sort of person who fusses about the precise arrangement of my desk drawers. I like my life carefully organized. I like security. But again and again I confront the fact that ultimately there is no absolute security in my life, no point at which I can say, "Everything is settled, everything is accomplished, finished, nailed down tight." And to know that is very, very frightening.

Being a creature is a scary business, which is why most of us spend so much time and energy denying that we are one. We try to cover over the fact of being a creature by achievement, by organization of our lives, by attempting to rest secure on something that we know we control. But all

23 *Illusion of control,*

these efforts finally fail us, and when they do, we are plunged back into deeper and deeper nervousness or anxiety about being a creature.

When I was a graduate student at the University of Chicago, I had an experience which was a great shock. I realized I hadn't the foggiest notion why I should pray. I don't mean that I had "a crisis of faith." It was more a crisis of usefulness. I wasn't sure why I should pray, what purpose it served. If God already knew everything—all my hopes and fears and needs—then God did not need to hear about them from me. So why should I bore God and myself by telling God what God already knew? What could I say in prayer that was necessary or even important to say?

It occurred to me that if I were going to find out what prayer is about, I should look first to the classic Christian prayer, the prayer the Lord taught his disciples. And so for several months I prayed nothing but the Lord's Prayer. I must have prayed it a hundred times some days. Day after day after day, I prayed those words trying to come to some insight into what the words mean. Why is it that Jesus thought that this prayer was what his disciples ought to say to his Father? Gradually I came to see that the Lord's Prayer really comes down to two statements repeated in a number of parallel ways. The first half of the prayer, when we pray that God's name be hallowed, that God's kingdom come, and that God's will be done in heaven and on earth, is simply the petition that God be everything God is: _may God be God_. The second half of the prayer, when we pray for physical sustenance, for forgiveness, and to be preserved from temptation and delivered from evil, is simply the request that I may be what I am: _may I be your creature_. The Lord's Prayer may be paraphrased, I think, "May God be God, and may I be a creature."

The more I thought about this, the more I recognized that the great petition of all Christian prayer is that everything be what it is. We pray that God be the fullness of God, and that we may be what it is to be creatures, i.e. fully dependent upon God. And that is the purpose of prayer: to celebrate the goodness, the rightness of precisely what we find so frightening—being a creature. We must come to the point of accepting that we are creatures, and prayer is the celebration of the fact.

In Genesis the very first thing we are told about being a creature is that God regards our creatureliness as good (Gen 1:31). That is immensely important in the Jewish and Christian traditions: God's judgment on what God has created is that it is good. In the wonderfully dramatic story of the beginning of all things in Genesis 1—the story of the six days of creation and God's sabbath rest—we are told again and again that God sees that creation is good (Gen 1:4, 10, 12, 18, 21, 25 and 31). In that story, for the first five and a half days of the week of creation, the pattern is, "God said, 'Let there be...,' and there was..., and God saw that it was good." The emphasis is on God's utter sovereignty over creation.

Creating costs God no effort; God can knock off a firmament and separate dry land from the seas and bring into being all manner of living things without breaking a sweat—just "Let it be," and it is. But there is a break in the pattern when, on the afternoon of the sixth day, God comes to create human beings. For the first time, the story depicts God deliberating about what and how to create. And for the first time, God uses a blueprint. That blueprint is God's self: "Let us make the human being in our image and likeness" (Gen 1:26). What an extraordinary claim about the value of human beings, that we are modeled on God. And then, on the afternoon of the sixth day, at the climax of creation, Genesis tells us that God looked at all that had been made and saw, as the Hebrew text puts it, "that it was very, very good." To be a creature, and especially to be a human creature, is quite wonderful indeed, if Genesis is to be believed.

embrace our humanity & celebrate us

II. THE TEMPTATION TO DENY THE GOODNESS OF BEING CREATURE

I suggest that this story in Genesis 1 provides the context for understanding the story in Genesis 3, the story of the entry of evil into creation. What appears in chapter 3 is anxiety about the value of being a creature and rejection of the goodness of human beings. Recall the first temptation (Gen 3:5), "Eat this and you will be like God." Granted, Adam and Eve did not have the advantage of having read chapter 1. Had they, presumably they would have noticed that they are like God, that they had been created in the divine image and likeness. But enter the serpent who tells them, in effect, "You're not like God."

Being human is a wretched business: barely born when you start the pain of teething and learning to walk and talk, being subject to parents and teachers, going through the labor of study and learning, the awkwardness and embarrassment of adolescence, trying to discern a vocation, taking on the burdens of marriage and parenthood and making a living, worrying about the children and having them grow up and leave home, aging and losing friends, eyes getting weak and teeth falling out and hair disappearing, body getting frail and memory slipping away and, at long last, death. And this is supposed to be good! Being a creature is frightful. Be like God! Being God is good, and being a creature is not. The essence of the first temptation is to reject the goodness of creatureliness: be God or don't be at all! And, alas, we fall for that temptation.

According to Genesis 3, the root of evil in our world is the inability of our world to accept itself for what it is. Evil enters through the refusal of creatures to be creatures. Evil arises from the decision that, unless we are God, we are trash. There has been a good deal in the Christian tradition over the centuries about the last judgment. But since God is unchanging and eternal, I suspect that the last judgment will prove to be a repetition of the first judgement, which was, you recall, that God, having reviewed all creation, judged that it was very, very good. The refusal to accept and celebrate the goodness of being a creature is the rejection of the first judgement of God. The difference between the first judgment and the last is that, at the end of salvation history, we will finally accept and assent to the First Judgment. It is very, very good to be a creature, but we still find it immensely difficult to accept that goodness; being creatures makes us nervous.

We are nervous because we do not like being limited—in strength, in knowledge, in wisdom, in talent and, ultimately, in time—and we do not like being dependent. And however hard we try, however much we distract our attention and divert our minds, we cannot deny that finally we are not in control of our own lives. And we are frightened by that. All too often, we move in one of two directions. Either we try desperately to make ourselves independent, we take the serpent's suggestion and make a mad dash to be God, or we admit that we are not God and hate it. We deny the goodness of creatureliness and live lives of quiet desperation and sometimes of clamorous and destructive desperation. Coming to grips with the rightness of our own finite being, I suggest, lies at the very heart of what the Christian tradition means by salvation, reconciliation, and holiness.

From this perspective, the whole scriptural story is the revelation of the mystery hidden from all generations but now revealed (Col 1:26). What is that mystery, the great surprise of God's will? The mystery of God's purpose is that while ever since the entry of sin, we have been in a mad dash to become God, God has decided to become human. While we reject being limited, finite, creatures, i.e. being human, the one whose state was divine, in the words of the hymn which St. Paul quoted in Philippians, "did not cling to his equality with God but emptied himself to assume the condition of a servant, becoming human as all other human beings" (Phil 2:6–7). No wonder Paul thought the mystery breathtaking!

The claim that being human is so deeply good, so astonishingly precious, that God has chosen to take on humanity, is the ultimate affirmation that God looks at creation and sees that it is very, very good.

EXPERIENCING THE MYSTERY OF NOT BEING GOD

God thinks being human is so good, God has chosen to be human, too. And who am I to dispute the divine taste?

Every year the church begins its annual communal retreat, the season of Lent, by asking us to consider on the First Sunday of Lent the synoptic gospels' stories of the temptations of the Lord. Those stories are a replaying of Genesis 3. Scripture allows the devil only one good line, and the old serpent tries it again and again and again: "Eat this and be like God." It is evil's one great plot, but it is a devastatingly effective one. And the devil plays it one more time in the stories in Matthew's and Luke's gospels about the Lord's temptations. Having fasted forty days and nights in the desert, Jesus is hungry (Mt 4:2; Lk 4:2). And at that moment of creaturely weakness, the tempter offers his usual pitch: "If you are the Son of God, command these stones to become bread" (Mt 4:3; Lk 4:3), i.e. "If you are not merely human, if you are equal to God, then snap your fingers and turn stones into bread. Creatures, finite human beings, they might have to go hungry in the desert, but not you. Why ever would you want to be hungry? Come, come, let's not be foolish: if you are the Son of God, act like the Son of God." Do you hear the echo of the serpent in Eden? Being God is good; being human is not. Reject your humanity, your creatureliness, and be God. But, unlike what happened in Genesis 3, this time the temptation is rejected. "It is written: 'Not by bread alone does a human being live'" (Lk 4:4; Mt 4:4). Notice the emphasis on humanity and Jesus' identification of himself as human.

The second temptation, at least in Matthew's account (the gospel of Luke inverts the order of the second and third temptations of Matthew's version), finds the tempter bringing Jesus to the top of the temple in Jerusalem: "If you are the Son of God, leap off; for it is written, 'He will commit you to angels' care,' and 'They will bear you up on their hands, lest you strike your foot on a stone'" (Mt 4:6; Lk 4:9–11). "So, you want to identify with human beings, eh? You want to communicate to creatures your message? You'll have to tramp up and down dusty roads in Galilee and Judea, talk and persuade and cajole and come up with parables and snappy examples. And then some will get it and some won't. Some will buy it, some will reject it. Some will accept it initially and then fall away. Some may even end up denying you or betraying you. Why not manifest your divinity: jump off the roof of the temple, and angels will bear you up. You'll WOW Jerusalem. Everyone will rush to hear what you have to say. If you are the Son of God, act like the Son of God. Don't try dealing with them as creature to creatures. Act like God, and overwhelm these poor little creatures. In the long run, it will make your mission more effective, for you will find that they really don't want a fellow creature; they want God." And Jesus refuses, for "you shall not put the Lord your

God to the test" (Mt 4:7; Lk 4:12). Once again, notice that Jesus insists on living by faith, like other human beings.

So, off to the highest mountain in the world from which all the kingdoms of the earth can be seen. (It is interesting to observe that for the gospel writers the world was flat: if one can get up high enough one can see the edges.) And so, the third temptation (in Matthew, the second in Luke): "All this will I give you if you pay me homage" (Mt 4:9; Lk 4:6–7). "You want to save the world, Jesus? A noble ambition. And from whom do you intend to save it? Me? No need: I'll give it to you. Here it is— a present. Just ask. Simple recognition, that's all I ask. Deal with me as God to demon. Drop this pose of finiteness and go back to being God!" And Jesus refuses because only God is to be worshiped (Mt 4:10; Lk 4:8). Once again, notice that Jesus will do what creatures do, i.e. worship God.

Matthew ends his story there: "The devil left him, and angels came and ministered to him" (Mt 4:11). But Luke concludes his account with a much more ominous line: "And when the devil had exhausted his temptations, he left him until there would be a better opportunity" (Lk 4:13). Luke warns that the devil will be back. The temptations are not over yet in Luke's gospel. The devil has only one card to play, and if it does not work now, then he will play it later in the game at a better time. And Luke clearly signals us when that better time arrives.

The last temptation of Christ in Luke's gospel takes place in Gethsemane just before his arrest. In Matthew's and Mark's gospels, when Jesus arrives at the garden with his disciples, he tells them to be seated while he goes apart to pray (Mt 26:36; Mk 14:32). But in Luke's gospel, he warns them, "Pray so that you may not be tempted" (Lk 22:40), for the hour of the last and greatest temptation has arrived. Then Jesus prays in such anguish that "his sweat became like great drops of blood" (Lk 22:44): "Father, if you will, remove this cup from me" (Lk 22:42). The last temptation is the horror of the ultimate reality of our finiteness, our creatureliness: death. For that is what happens to creatures—we come to an end, we die. "Jesus, you've done a very impressive job. I didn't think you would carry off being human as fully as you have. But now we come to the crunch, the bottom line. Creatures die, Jesus, sometimes all alone and rejected, sometimes in great pain, sometimes in torture. Come now, you don't want to die. And you don't have to: go back to being God and forget this nonsense about being human." But Jesus prays, "Father, let not my will but yours be done" (Lk 22:42). And then an angel comes to minister to him—the sign from Matthew's gospel that temptation has been surmounted. The last temptation is the anxiety of death when Jesus comes face to face with creatureliness.

The gospel of John has no story of Jesus' anguished prayer in

Gethsemane. But the author of the fourth gospel dramatically presents the same struggle of Jesus with death as the ultimate mark of being a creature. The last temptation becomes in John the story of the raising of Lazarus (Jn 11:1–44). In the fourth gospel this story marks the first occasion when Jesus confronts death. In the synoptic gospels, we find earlier stories about Jesus encountering death: the raising of Jairus' daughter and of the son of the widow at Naim, and Jesus' reception of the news of John the Baptist's death. But those stories do not appear in John's gospel. Prior to the Lazarus story, the closest Jesus comes to a direct confrontation with death in the fourth gospel is when he is requested to cure the official's son at Capernaum, who is described as being at the point of death (Jn 4:47). But even that healing is "at a distance," i.e. Jesus does not meet the dying boy himself.

The first time that he directly meets death with its pain and grief and loss is when his friend Lazarus dies. And what is his response? He is "deeply troubled" (Jn 11:33). He is moved to tears (v 35). He sighs from the depths of his being (v 38). I suggest to you that the fourth gospel wants to show us that Jesus is not moved alone because of Martha's and Mary's grief or because of his friend's death, but by death itself, including especially his own death. This is the story in John's gospel of Jesus' confronting what it is to be a creature. The tomb where Lazarus has been buried is described as a cave sealed with a stone, reminiscent of the description of Jesus' own tomb later. As at Gethsemane, Jesus will pray as he stands before this tomb. He has been warned about opening the tomb: "Lord, the stench will be terrible. He's been four days in the tomb." Jesus will be only three days in the tomb. Lazarus' case is made even worse; he is not just dead, he is as dead as you can get, dead and decaying. But even confronting death in all its darkness and dissolution, Jesus remains confident in the Father: "I know you always hear me" (Jn 11:42).

Earlier in the fourth gospel, when the first disciples follow Jesus, they reply to his inquiring what they seek by asking where he dwells; Jesus responds, "Come and see" (Jn 1:38–39). In the Lazarus story, when Jesus asks the mourners where the dead man has been placed, they respond, "Come and see" (Jn 11:34). The balance is pointed: the Lord of life invites us to come and see where he dwells and shows us the fullness of life; we invite the Lord to come and see where we dwell and take him to the tomb. He shows us the glory of God, and we show him what it is like to be a creature. And he chooses to be one, even to death, even to death on a cross.

III. "O HAPPY FAULT"

Lent begins with our being confronted by these stories of Jesus' temptations to abandon creatureliness and reject finiteness, and it ends six weeks later with the members of the community renewing their baptismal promises. For Lent is not first and foremost a period of penance; it is most importantly a communal retreat during which we are asked to consider what our baptism meant and how we are living up to or failing the commitments we made. At the end of Lent we are invited once again to renew those commitments when we renew our baptismal vows. All over the world, the members of the church renew their baptismal vows at the Easter vigil or at the masses on Easter morning. And those vows are our rejection of the temptation against the goodness of being creatures, the temptation which Adam and Eve accepted in the garden and over which Jesus triumphed in the desert.

After we renounce evil and sin, we are asked to make three vows which are phrased as three statements of faith: "Do you believe in God the Father, the maker of heaven and earth? Do you believe in Jesus Christ, God's Son, who became a human being, lived and suffered and died and was raised again by the Father and who now reigns in glory? Do you believe in the holy spirit and in the church?" To hear these questions as requests for assent to matters of fact is to misunderstand them and to misunderstand the importance of our baptism completely. Anyone can agree that these things are so—there is a God, Christ was sent by God, the Spirit is still active in the world. The issue is: What do they mean for us? Why must we make these statements of faith *as promises*?

Consider the first vow. We are asked whether we believe in God who is the creator of all. That means that we are asked whether we believe that there is a maker of all that exists, that existence has a purpose and a meaning, that I have a purpose to my existence, *and that I do not determine what that purpose is.* The world was not made by me; I am not made by me. I am not the meaning-giver and ultimate determiner of my own life. There is a meaning-giver to my life, and I am not it. My life is not for me because I did not originate it nor do I decide what it is for or about. There are many, many, many people who either deny that life has a purpose or assert that they are the ones who determine what their life is for and how it should be lived. And we are asked to affirm that they are wrong, that life's meaning, including our own lives' meaning, is not given by us, that we are creatures and so are not the ultimate controllers, judges, or directors of our lives. Do you believe that? Do you live that way? Can you live that way? Think long and hard before answering "yes."

Consider the second vow. Having announced that we are not meaning-givers in our own lives, we are asked whether we believe that nevertheless what we are is so good that the One who is the meaning-giver, God, has chosen to become what we are. That is the meaning of the incarnation. God has created humanity so wonderfully that God "did not cling to his equality with God but emptied himself to assume the condition of a servant, becoming human as all other human beings" (Phil. 2:6–7). Do you believe that you are of such extraordinary value that God has chosen to become what you are rather than remain in the form of God? And if you do believe that about your humanity and the humanity of every other human being, then must you not treat every human being, including yourself, as of infinite value? Do you believe that? Do you live that way? Can you live that way? Once again, think long and hard before answering "yes."

Consider the third vow. The living God who is the meaning-giver of our lives and who has chosen to be one with us is still present in our world and in our experience; that is what we mean when we affirm that the Holy Spirit of God has been poured into the world. But notice where we say that Spirit is to be found: in the church, i.e. in the community. That means that the Spirit of God now dwells not first and foremost in you or in me but in us. God is to be encountered in our community with others. Can we arch-individualists—for all Americans are arch-individualists—affirm that God is not found first in the depths of my heart but in my life and work and struggle with other people? It is one thing to affirm the existence of God and my need for God; it is quite another to affirm that this means that I need you and her and him and them, and that without all of you I cannot find the Spirit of God. But that is what the third vow asks us to affirm. Do you believe that? Do you live that way? Can you live that way? And still again, think long and hard before answering "yes."

There is a further dimension to consider about our creatureliness, our limitedness, a dimension which is given extraordinary statement at the start of the Easter vigil during which we renew our baptismal vows. In Book 10 of his *Confessions*, St. Augustine raises an interesting question. In the previous nine books he has recounted his life until the time of his mother's death and his conversion, and much of what he has recounted he now regards as sinful. But if he has been wringing his hands for nine whole books about how wicked his earlier life had been, why bother to remember it and, even more, record it? If he has sinned and those sins have now been forgiven by God, as Augustine believes they have, then should they not simply be forgotten? Should they not be put out of mind as something shameful, something to be rejected? Why lavish such effort on recalling what he now rejects, not to mention such glorious literary skill?

Augustine's answer to the question is immensely insightful. He decides that it is important that he remember his past, including his sin, both because that sin now in recollection provides occasion for glorifying God's mercy and goodness, and because his sin is part of *his* past, a past which has brought him to the point at which he can glorify God. This Augustinian insight has been enshrined in the *Exsultet*, the great proclamation of the joy of the resurrection sung at the Easter vigil on Holy Saturday night: "O happy fault, O necessary sin of Adam!" What an odd phrase, "O happy fault." The church seems to celebrate the fall of humanity into sin. But it does so because the meaning of that fall has been forever changed by the action of God in Christ's life, death and destiny.

Now, seen in the light of Easter, we can call our sinfulness a "happy fault" because it gives us the opportunity to celebrate the forgiving love of God and tells us who we are in relation to God. We are the people who are always being forgiven. We are constantly the recipients of mercy. And therefore it is good that we, like Augustine, remember our moral limitedness and our constant dependence on God not only as creatures held in existence by the divine agape but as sinners forgiven by that self-giving love.

Recognizing ourselves as creatures means that we have to come to grips not only with the limits of our physical being but with the defects of our moral goodness. We are not creatures in the abstract; we are creatures with concrete pasts, individually and communally. And those pasts are not histories of pure and perfect agapic love. Frequently, they are dark and sometimes brutal tales of selfishness and hatred and deep despair. And so we must accept the fact that we are all, in one way or another, morally tarnished. That is not to be regarded as an embarrassing and unfortunate flaw. It must be turned into what Augustine saw it could be, an occasion of joyful acceptance of our dependence upon God for forgiveness as well as existence. It brings me back again to the central Christian prayer, which I have suggested can be paraphrased, "May you be God; may I be your creature." The discovery of the goodness of creatureliness does not remove the experience of discomfort in being a creature, however. One classic way of naming that deep discomfort is restlessness. We should talk in Chapter 3 about how we can be both restless and joyful.

The Blessedness of Limits
RESPONSE BY JAN PILARSKI

When Michael talks about the questions of what constitutes security and of how to find purpose and meaning outside one's self, I am moved to reflect on the ways that being a parent forces me to consider my own creatureliness. Like Michael, I too am a person who likes order and the ability to plan and project—those disciplines have always seemed a source of stability and security for me.

But perhaps the first thing a new parent discovers is that the birth of a child removes any semblance of a schedule or routine. Here is this amazing newborn, totally dependent on your care, birthed out of the shared conviction that love and life are indeed good and holy. Yet the rhythms and needs of that baby are so clearly different from our adult priorites and preoccupations. Shortly after the birth seven years ago of my first child, Christopher, I remember being struck by the contrasts and juxtapositions in my life because of now having a child. One week earlier I was organizing tenants outside Washington, D.C. to confront their landlord about sub-standard living conditions; the next week I was nursing Christopher every few hours and providing for all of his other basic needs. How wonderful and yet radically different my life became now that I was a mother!

In giving birth to Christopher and his brothers David and Kevin, I have experienced a sense of expansiveness and joy because of the physical act of giving life, but I have also encountered my limitations in a very profound and humbling way. When Chris was born I rebelled against the fact that my life had changed so much. I struggled with the temptation Michael describes as wanting to remain in control of our lives.

I resented the fact that my husband Jay's life seemed to change so little after Christopher's birth and mine had been turned upside-down. Jay had both his work and his time with Chris, while I felt that continuing to work intensely was draining me of energy and time with my child. I longed for a society where both parents could share equally in raising their children, while respecting the needs for both men and women to be engaged in meaningful activity outside the home as well. At the same time, on an individual level I wanted desperately to acquire some control over all the parts of my life that were no longer exclusively mine. With the insights now provided by Michael, I see that what I wanted then was to turn stones into bread. I wrestled with the temptation to deny my limitations and forget my creatureliness.

Jan Pilarski with her children David, Kevin, and Chris

Praying about the changes that had happened in my life since becoming a mother, I realized my own need to come to terms with parenthood and simply accept that my life would always be different than before, both in ways that I enjoyed and in aspects I felt less comfortable with. The words of Ecclesiasteses pointed me toward a new understanding of my creatureliness in relationship to mothering a child. I perceived a time for all things within the span of one's life, but realized that not all of those things need happen at the same time. I began to consider my time with my children—indeed, the ordinary experience of each day—as a prayer that I lived, challenging me to see God in the faces of those with whom I shared my life and my brokenness.

With the birth of David two years after Christopher, we definitely encountered our finitude as we juggled the needs of a toddler and baby! Wondering how to provide the attention and care two young ones needed simultaneously, the first year of David's life seemed such a whirlwind. But the physical effort of caring for them both was compensated by watching the two of them interact. They hugged each other, laughed, and were always patting each other's heads; they loved nothing more than to play side by side. Though our lives were more constrained in external ways, we found the bonds of love and friendship developing between our sons to be wonderful indeed.

It was during this joyous first year of David's life, however, that a new chapter opened up for us in our parenting and we encountered our own limits in deeper and more unexpected ways. I began to notice that David's pace of development as an infant was so different than Christopher's had been. At $2\frac{1}{2}$ years of age, Christopher's speech was delayed and he had difficulty playing with children other than David. He did not give other people eye contact and was oblivious to the presence of others. I was confused because many of these behaviors had not been a problem when Christopher was younger. What was happening to my son? Where was God during a time I felt hopelessly alone?

In the next year we were to discover that Chris had autism—a disability that involves often severe impairments in social and communication skills. Like many other autistic children, Chris has difficulty adjusting to change and has a very hard time knowing how to play with others.

I did much of my grieving and adjusting during the year leading up to the diagnosis. What was most painful for me was being in situations where I would see typical two or three year old children, and realized all the things they did compared to Christopher. I had dreams of Chris singing songs, going to birthday parties and having a best friend. I imagined him running in a field casting off his autism, unencumbered;

again, the temptation to turn stones into bread and Chris into the child
he was not.

Reflecting on Michael's thoughts on prayer and creatureliness, I
resonate so strongly with his understanding of prayer as the petition that
everything be what it is. When I learned the name for Christopher's
diagnosis, I thought silently to myself: "So that is what this is." And I felt
that although Chris now had a name for what affected him, he was still
the same beautiful child I had loved before. When I got that diagnosis I
thought of him as still the boy who smiled with all the love he had inside
himself—and I embraced who he is, not what he would be in a perfect
world. It was then that I understood God was not a remote observer, but
present in the love that bound Chris and me to each other.

Life with Chris has taught me so much about the intersection between
limits, goodness and sharing our gifts. I was struck by the reflection that
limits are not only part of being human, but good because they allow us
to see who we are in relationship to God. One of the ways that insight
becomes meaningful for me is through the questions Chris constantly
poses about why things happen. Because change is hard for him to
accept, he wants to know things like where the day goes when it's night
and what happens to 1994 when that year is over.

I have honestly never thought of those things, but my reaction is to
marvel at the mystery of God and the wonder of creation which Chris
highlights through his questions. It is then that I realize how much we
take for granted, how much we assume about the way things work, how
much our limits push us to search for the Spirit and perceive that God's
ways and our ways are ever distinct. Christopher's example teaches me
that limits have the potential to be transformative; not to turn the bad
into good, but providing us the space to discover our dependence on
God and where our true security rests.

In our situation, I have had to learn to let go of my dreams and hopes
much earlier than most parents would in their child's life. But what
many people perceive as constraints I see as opportunities to stretch our
notion of what constitutes goodness. My struggles and questions have
prodded me to consider the incarnation as something which our family
experiences as we live our lives each day. For when I imagine Christ
becoming human and accepting our weaknesses, I have an image of him
being present especially with children like Chris—acknowledging their
special gifts, accepting them for who they are, taking the time to speak to
them and play with them, emptying his life for them, bearing humilia-
tion through the sacrifice of his death upon the cross.

About a year ago I recalled the meaning of the name Christopher and
the beautiful story of St. Christopher bearing the Christ child across the

water. And I thought of Christopher in the tangle of his autism bearing Christ to our family, of us encountering God in what happens between us on a daily basis. "So that is what this is," I thought. Although I am learning to realize more and more what little control I have over my life in the large sense, I see my life stretching out before me as a prayer in which I am called to simply say, "May everything be what it is."

Questions

1. What is difficult about being human? What is wonderful about being human, and utterly dependent on God?

2. How does knowing that God chose to enter fully into the human state through the person of Jesus Christ enhance your understanding of "creatureliness"?

3. What is the meaning of death? Look carefully at the story of Lazarus in John's gospel (11:1–44). What is Jesus' response to death? Mary's? Martha's?

4. What are the three affirmations in the baptismal vows which are renewed every year at the Easter vigil? Explain as if to the class how we are to understand each of these?

5. What connections do you see between Jan Pilarski's reflections on human limitedness and your own experience?

Journal Question

6. Select five of your favorite stories from the gospels. Examine the characters in each of these stories and write a few paragraphs about each character, describing each one's creatureliness. Some examples are the disciples Peter and Thomas, the woman at the well, Zacchaeus, the woman caught in adultery, the disciples caught in a storm at sea.

3
THE JOURNEY OF RESTLESSNESS: THE SEARCH FOR GOD

You made us for yourself, and our hearts are restless until they rest in you.
—St. Augustine, *Confessions* 1,1

I. HUMANS ARE FUNDAMENTALLY RESTLESS

My hero is St. Augustine. He is, in my opinion, the most extraordinary mind that the Christian tradition has yet seen. And probably the single most famous, most often quoted line he ever wrote is found at the outset of his *Confessions*. Speaking to God (and the whole of the *Confessions* is addressed to God), he wrote, "You made us for yourself and our hearts are restless until they rest in you." This gets to the heart of what it is to be a human being.

If I were to choose a single characteristic to describe human life, I would pick restlessness. Have you ever found a dog that wanted to be a cat or a cow that wanted to be a tree? But have you ever known a human being who didn't want to be someone or something more—who didn't want to be more, do more, know more, have more, feel more? Every human being is fundamentally restless and dissatisfied. We are always hungry. At the center of our being is an endlessly nagging sense of "Yes, yes, yes, but more." There is never a moment at which we are at rest fully and completely. This is why Augustine's description is so insightful. But the insight is complemented by his great discovery, the recognition that this restlessness is the best thing about us.

Far from being an evil, far from having to conclude that we have to still the restlessness at the core of our being, to let it simmer down so that finally we are at peace, Augustine came to recognize that we must stoke the restlessness. We must keep ourselves restless. We would be absolutely lost if we were not restless. Why? Because our restlessness is what drives us to God at last, if we are faithful to it.

One way to read the *Confessions* is as a book about Augustine's discovery that the restlessness which he thought was a curse is in fact the great blessing. It was his restless heart which led him to God. Our restlessness is the great blessing because it is what keeps us from becoming idolaters. Once one reaches a point at which he or she can say, "This is it. *Now* I'm satisfied. I want nothing else. I'm finally at peace with this person or thing or idea or experience or place or time. This"—whatever it may be—"is all I need," one has fallen into idolatry. For what one is really saying is, "This person, thing, idea, experience, place, time, has completely satisfied me. It has given my heart peace. I neither need nor want anything else. This"—whatever it may be—"is God." What Augustine saw so brilliantly was that what keeps us from idolatry, what keeps us from "selling out cheap" for something less than God, is the restlessness of our hearts. And so his advice was: by all means, stay restless.

But in various ways all of us try to still the restlessness. We may try to still it with very destructive things—drugs and alcohol and sexual indulgence. We may try to still it with very marvelous things—service to others and knowledge and marriage and children. We may try to still it with prayer and sacrifice and dedication to our vocations. But whatever we try to still our restless hearts with, we must realize that none of them work. None of them ever satisfy the hunger. The hunger, the restlessness drives us on.

Often we attempt to resolve that restlessness once and for all through a deep relationship with some particular person. When I have the opportunity to speak with couples preparing to marry or who are married or who have been married, I suggest to them that one of the most destructive things they can encounter in marriage is the attempt to make one another effectively into God. "She's all I need!" "He's all I want!" No! You need a lot more than her or him. And he or she needs a lot more than you. The moment you say "This one's all I need," you have said, in effect, "This one's God. This person will finally resolve the restlessness of my heart. At long last, I won't feel the need for something else because I've got her or him." That might work if he or she dies on the honeymoon, or if you do, but if the relationship lasts any longer than a very brief honeymoon, you will discover to your dismay that it hasn't worked. You will remain restless and hungry. You will find yourself ruefully admitting that he or she is not all you want. And, alas, that is the moment when so many marriages hit enormous problems. We cannot cast another person in the role no one should try to fill: the role of God. When the other person fails to play the part successfully, we end up feeling betrayed: "Why isn't he what I thought he was?" "Why doesn't she satisfy me?" And the answer is that he or she is not what you expected him or her to be—namely, God.

All friendships are healthy so long as we recognize that these relationships are a partial experience of the absolute love which is God. When we try to move a relationship with another person from a partial experience to the whole experience of *agape* which is God, it becomes destructive, even demonic. When we discover that the relationship fails to satisfy our every hope and dream and desire we have an opportunity to uncover within ourselves the fundamental restlessness of our hearts. We smash an idol when we discover that it was just too small a god. If you can live with that discovery, then you have the basis for a genuinely joyful relationship. If you do not idolize the other people but love them for whom they are and not for whom you would like them to be, you have a friendship grounded in grace. The sense of loss often experienced in relationships is the disappointed realization that no relationship is "the ultimate relationship."

II. THE SEARCH: SATISFACTION OR JOY?

If Augustine's account of his experience in his *Confessions* is a true and universal one, what is the worst fate that can befall us? Satisfaction. A premature and too easy fulfillment stills the restless. The hungry heart is filled. So the claim that we are satisfied means that we have found God. And too facile a claim to have found God may mean that something demonic has found us.

The delightful and, I think, quite wonderful American poet, Marianne Moore, has in one of my favorite among her poems "What Are Years?" the splendidly accurate lines, "satisfaction is a lowly/ thing, how pure a thing is joy." Exactly right! The contrast is between joy and satisfaction or happiness. Satisfaction or happiness is conditioned by a thousand external circumstances; whether one had a good night's sleep, whether one has a cold, whether one's breakfast was cold, whether one's shoes are too tight, whether one has an exam the next day, whether one has just had an argument with a close friend, whether one's car needs repairs—all sorts of things affect whether or not one feels happy at any particular moment. Joy, by contrast, is impervious to all such issues. This is why, within the Christian tradition, we speak of joy as one of the fruits of the Holy Spirit. No one has ever claimed that the Holy Spirit makes us happy, but the Spirit does make us joyful. The Holy Spirit does not lead us to satisfaction. Indeed, if Augustine is right, what makes us satisfied is a demon and must be exorcised. One of the marks of the Holy Spirit's presence is that the Spirit makes us dissatisfied. The Holy Spirit keeps us saying, "Yes, yes, yes, but more." The Holy Spirit does not let us rest.

In John's gospel the Spirit is called the "Paraclete," a difficult word to translate. There is no exact English translation for the Greek "Paraclete." Sometimes it is translated as "advocate," i.e. someone who speaks for another, sometimes as "defender," i.e. someone who acts on one's behalf, one's counselor. But perhaps the closest we can get to the meaning of the word is "the one who spurs runners on in a race." The Paraclete is like an athlete's trainer. The Paraclete stands on the side of the track and encourages the runners, "You can do it! Go for it! Go for the gold!" So the Paraclete is the spur that drives us on. What a fascinating word to describe the Spirit! The Spirit is the one who pushes us on. Far from satisfying us, the Spirit is the one who spurs us forward. So, in Mark's gospel we first hear that the Spirit is at work when we read that "the Spirit drove Jesus out into the desert" (Mk 1:12). The Spirit's first appearance is in driving Jesus forward. The Spirit keeps saying, "Go further, go further." The Spirit does not offer happiness. The Spirit does not offer satisfaction. What the Spirit offers is joy.

What does joy mean? Let me turn to another of my heroes, Jonathan Edwards, the great eighteenth-century Puritan pastor, preacher and theologian. In 1755, Edwards wrote a book entitled *The Nature of True Virtue*. The word virtue does not mean for us what it meant for Edwards and his readers in the eighteenth century. We might be closer to his meaning were we to take true virtue as true sanctity or holiness. He defined what he called true virtue and what we will call true holiness in a splendid phrase: "the consent of being to being." I know that, at first glance, this seems a rather dry way of describing holiness, and so you may well ask, "What's so splendid about that?" Let me suggest to you that what Edwards was after was not only the consent of human beings to Being, i.e. to God, nor even their consent to being in general, i.e. the way things are. Rather, he was thinking also of each particular human being saying "yes" to being that particular human being.

True holiness is, according to Edwards, the consent of finite, creaturely, unfulfilled being to being finite, creaturely and unfulfilled. True holiness is coming to the point at which one can say, "I am unfulfilled. My heart is restless, and I choose that it shall remain restless. For it is good that my heart is hungry." True holiness requires that this unfulfilled creature say, "Yes, it is good to be an unfulfilled creature." This is what it means for a being to consent to being. Holiness consists in bringing one's thought and will into line with God's judgment. And we know God's judgment on creation—including the creatures that you and I are: "God looked at it and saw that it was very, very good" (Gen 1:31).

This, I suggest, is the central ingredient of joy. When I can say, "It is a very, very good thing that I am I," knowing that "I" am not fulfilled, not trying to substitute some imaginary "I" for the real "I," not claiming that it is good that I am I because I am the center, the meaning, the maker of the universe, in short, not making "I" God, then not only do I consent to my own finite being, I rejoice in it. There are lots of limitations which constitute my concrete being—physical, spiritual, intellectual, moral, temporal—but I choose to be this limited being. God has chosen to make me, and I agree with God that it is good.

Thus joy appears when I can say that this pudgy little body is not likely to become the world's greatest pole vaulter, nor this voice to sing *Siegfried* at the Met, nor this talent to produce a poem which will eclipse Milton. Limitedness is both real and good. In all sorts of ways, our society tells us that limitation is irrelevant. Think of all those rather too-sweet inspirational made-for-television movies about people who have horrible accidents and then go on to demonstrate that the accidents did not matter at all. Not true. Were I to lose a leg, it is perfectly true that my life would not be over, that my value as a human being would certainly not be diminished, that I might achieve great deeds. But it is also true that I would not dance with the Bolshoi Ballet. Limitations do matter. And the denial of limitedness is not heroism; it is the failure of finite being to consent to being finite, to being a creature.

The fact is that I am who I am. There are limits to my wisdom and my knowledge and my strength and my courage and my patience and my love. I am something, but I am not everything. And I am good. I am also hungry to be more than I am. I want to grow and expand and develop, but I do not have to lay any claim to be all-wise and fully loving, completely courageous and perfectly powerful, before I can say, "Being Himes is a good thing." Nor is this a facile and rather banal "I'm okay—you're okay" attitude. Actually, what I mean is more: "I'm not at all okay and you're probably a good deal worse, but we're good." This being can consent to being this being. And that is where joy enters in—not satisfaction with oneself, which Marianne Moore rightly calls "a lowly thing," but joy, and "how pure a thing is joy."

III. RESTLESSNESS AND GUILT

There is a possibility for misunderstanding the restlessness of the heart, and that is to see it as the result of guilt. The worst possible motive for the Christian life—and for serving others—is guilt. It is one thing to recognize one's own sinfulness, but it is quite another to regret one's past. I do not care what your past was or wasn't, never regret it; after all, it got you to where you are now. Whatever got you to this present moment when you are considering the meaning of your life with God and your service of others is a good thing. Earlier we spoke of Augustine's willingness to celebrate his sinful past because without it he would not have come to the moment when he could write his *Confessions* and his daring praise of the sin of Adam and Eve as a "happy fault." Well, whatever has brought you to the point at which you too can give yourself away in service to others, and so come to the experience of God, is not to be rejected. Even if you now regard it as sinful and wrong, selfish and foolish, celebrate it as a "happy fault." For the past is always to be embraced; it is what has made the present possible. And if the present is a moment of insight or challenge, recognize that you would not be at this moment of insight had it not been for that past.

But this certainly does not mean that you should fail to be critical in your evaluation of the past or, for that matter, of the present. The consent of being to being does not mean that whatever is, is right. And the ability to celebrate one's past as a happy fault does not mean that one does not acknowledge that one has, indeed, been at fault. The celebration of finiteness does not entail blindness to evil in one's own life or in the world around one. Always remain critical. Thus your commitment to service of others may make you deeply uncomfortable. You may find that your work with the poor makes you very sensitive to the waste of money, resources, time and energy in your own life and the lives of those around you. The time you spend with the ill and dying, the aged and the lonely may well make you self-conscious about the level of comfort and secur', which you have taken for granted in your own life. You may h? to confront a lack of awareness and of compassion and the re .ty of blindness and sin in yourself and in our world. Recognize it, c nfront it, say it. Keep your critical judgment keen. But do not turn ,our critical awareness into guilt and allow that to be the motivating force of your service. And do not permit yourself the easy luxury of anger aimed at yourself or others. Do not self-righteously proclaim that your way of service to others is the only way in which one can be a Christian. It may very well be your way. But there may be other ways which are crucially important and immensely rich for other people. Do not absolutize your way of service, do not apologize for it, and do not make it a way of expiating guilt.

Living the Christian life should not be rooted in guilt. There are, I think, two good reasons to be Christian. One is given in chapter 6 of John's gospel. It is Peter's reply to Jesus' question when many of his hearers, having found his words too difficult to accept, turn away: "Are you going to go away, too?" And Peter answered, "Whom else can we go to? You have the words of eternal life" (Jn 6:67–68). One very good reason to be Christian is that, in one sense, we are stuck with it. There simply is not anything else in the world that makes as much sense. Even if I wanted something else to be the case, nothing else is. Nothing else deals more richly or truly with the depths of the mystery that I find in the depths of my own being and my restless heart. That is the first reason to be a Christian.

The second reason, which is where I hope you end up even if you start out from the first, is because living this life is a source of joy. You may not—indeed, I am quite sure you will not—find that a life of agapic love and service makes you happy and satisfied. It will not make you content or give you rest. But I think that it will exhilarate and energize you. It may kill you, but you will not die of boredom. You will find out who you are and who God is by giving yourself away in loving service to others. You may be driven to self-gift by the restlessness of your heart, and you will not find in such self-gift any easy stilling of that restlessness. You will run headlong into the sometimes brutal fact of your own limitedness and that of others, and if you are wise and fortunate, you will be able to rejoice in that encounter. You will find no fulfillment, no satisfaction. But so what? What a deadly fate fulfillment would be! And, after all, "satisfaction is a lowly/thing, how pure a thing is joy."

Shaking The Ground Beneath Our Feet
RESPONSE BY LOU NANNI

Sometimes we believe before we understand. In 1984, during my senior year at Notre Dame, I applied for a two year cross-cultural overseas mission experience in Santiago, Chile with the Holy Cross Associates program. During the interview process, I spoke about the need for suffering in my life. While I did not understand it in such terms then, I felt it necessary to *stoke my restlessness* as a means to growing closer to God.

Michael Himes' reflection on restlessness allows me to understand this period in my life much more clearly, and inspires me to remain vigilant to such temptations as security and fulfillment. Michael describes the great enemy in *The Confessions* as satisfaction or fulfillment. For if we become filled up, literally, we can no longer be open to God's truth and love. The reliability of a new car, job success and security, a good health and life insurance policy, a sound investment, the perfect relationship—all are temporal goals for which most of us strive in our daily lives. The catch is that spiritually they can delude us into feeling secure, safe,

Lou Nanni (center) with guests at the Center for the Homeless

prepared. Yet through our smallest cracks, which reveal the least bit of openness, enters the Holy Spirit, or what Michael describes as the *Paraclete*. In my life, this *Paraclete persists to spur me on in the race*. It is this restlessness which I so often curse, and at times lament, that allows me to grow in faith and love as a Christian.

Restlessness is predicated on truth. It involves fundamental questioning of one's own ways and beliefs. When Charles Darwin was exploring Chile over a century ago, he experienced a powerful earthquake, and his premise that the earth was immovable was literally shaken by the tremors beneath his feet. Chile did much the same for me. After four enjoyable and affirming years at Notre Dame, I was abruptly displaced, living in a Santiago shantytown under the ruthless dictatorship of a military regime. Distant from family and friends, I struggled with health problems as I adjusted to a new language, culture, political situation and socio-economic reality. Loneliness and self-doubt filled the spaces where pride and confidence had only recently dwelled.

Satisfaction and happiness, which Michael describes as conditioned by external circumstances, were for the first time in my life no longer present. I cried myself to sleep many nights thinking of the profound suffering which surrounded me in our neighborhood. Children not clothed adequately against the cold and rain. Students subjected to an educational system which was content to leave their God-given talents undeveloped. Teens and adults tortured, some to death, because they courageously stood for the truth. Masses of people who had lost belief in themselves and hope for the future. What was there to be happy about? In fact, I soon came to feel that I was as powerless as they to change this unjust reality, even for one lost soul. Or so it seemed.

Nobody ever said the Holy Spirit was going to make us happy, but it is going to make us joyful, Michael explains. In fact, the *Holy Spirit will make us unsatisfied*. I was unsatisfied and disgusted not so much by the military regime and its instruments of destruction as by the majority of individuals who cowardly acquiesced and remained indifferent before it. I also was distressed by the abrupt recognition of my own limitations. I realized to my horror that I was not going to become another Martin Luther King, Jr. Indeed, there were others in my community who were better listeners, more courageous and more faithful. I was unsatisfied, unhappy...and though I did not realize it, the Holy Spirit was at work.

While searching in vain for fulfillment and satisfaction, I found joy. I discovered hope in the common-day prophets all around me. People who had transformed suffering into joy. People who had found resurrection in their own crucifixion, and who shared it with others. A very poor family would invite me into their home and serve hot dogs, and a young child would inadvertently say, "This is the first time we've eaten meat in two years." Or it was a mother who learned that a couple of neighborhoods over, a young man had been tortured to death, and she would protest in the street before the armed forces knowing full well she could be orphaning her own children in the process. She knew it was the right course of action, that it had to be done, and her faith and shared pain with that mother nearby allowed her to rise above her fears and self-interest. If she did not act, she knew she could not expect anyone else to. This was joy, and I found it emerge through the cracks of broken lives, not from the satisfied and comfortable of this world.

The most challenging stage in the cross-cultural overseas mission experience is when the missioner returns home and begins to integrate the experience. I vacillated between two extremes. At the one end, I felt the need to be prophetic and critical, remaining true to the Chilean poor who had shaped and formed me. At the other end, I wanted to fit back into my own culture, with my own people, and within my own socio-economic background. Yet in my moments of comfort, I felt as if I had "sold out," and in times of prophetic witness I felt cynical and judgmental. As the pendulum swung between these two extremes, I soon conceded that I would never achieve that perfect balance for which I was searching. In fact, I discovered that this restlessness could become a creative force in my life. St. Augustine must have been watching over me with a wry smile.

The pendulum of restlessness continues to swing in my life today. As director of a full-service Center for the Homeless which houses and treats more than 100 homeless individuals every day, my restlessness is stoked on a regular basis. While the Center has received many accolades and considerable recognition nationally, we continue to meet more failure than success on a daily basis. The level of despair and the complexity of problems make for formidable odds. The work is not satisfying, but it is joyful. I cannot end a day feeling content for the fine presentation I delivered, or the wonderful report I prepared. Instead, at the end of each day I am overwhelmed by my limitations, and all the needs which go unmet. This places me in a position to reflect daily on two very important matters: one is *how much we need each other*, and the other is *how much we need God*. I no longer need to discipline myself to pray because I find myself in a position where I need prayer, for I have nowhere else to turn.

I am drawn to work with homeless individuals and families first and foremost because I need them. In fact, we need each other. If Christ were to enter the Center tomorrow in the face of a stranger and invite me to dinner, I would have to schedule him in a couple of weeks. If he were to invite one of the residents at the Center, however, they could readily dine that evening. Has it not always been the case that our prophets come from the margins of society with little vested in this world? Ruth, Job, John the Baptist, Augustine and Christ himself maintained lives characterized by profound restlessness and an openness to receive God's love and radiate it to others. If I am not at the margins myself, I at least want to be close to people who are. And the homeless continue to challenge and reveal to me the mysteries of God, helping me to grow in ways which I want and need as a Christian.

When Michael speaks of the temptation "to still the restlessness" in our lives, the first example he uses is within the relationship of marriage. At the time of this writing, I will be married in a few days. My fiancée and I read Michael's reflection on restlessness as part of our Pre-Cana preparation, for we fear settling into a marriage characterized by security and fulfillment. How can we together, and especially with children, continue to stoke the restlessness in our lives? It is profoundly challenging over the long haul to stay in that spot of loneliness, of restlessness, of longing, of unfulfillment, of not falling prey to satisfaction. It is awesome to think in such terms. We would be wise perhaps to borrow from the spirituality of Alcoholics Anonymous and tackle the challenge of restlessness one day at a time.

In the final analysis, I believe that a restless life open to God knows that even amidst great suffering and disillusionment, every moment we live presents an opportunity to love radically, to take a risk on behalf of another, to testify to the power of life over death. And that is very, very hopeful. It is joyful.

Questions

1. Why is it wonderful to be restless? How is restlessness productive? How is it destructive?

2. What is an idolatrous relationship? Give examples from the book and on your own.

3. What is guilt? How does it play a role in service? How is this unhealthy? What might be a more constructive way to enter into service to others?

4. In your own words, give two good reasons for being a Christian.

Journal Questions

5. Make a list of all the things you like about yourself. Write about the limitations you sometimes experience in becoming the person you most want to become. Share what you wrote with a close friend and write their responses afterward.

or

6. Reflect on all the past events of your life. You can do this in paragraph form, or you can draw a time line—low points on the line would represent the struggles you've had; high points would reflect the times when you felt really good about yourself. Looking over your personal biography, what common thread can you find in all of these experiences? How have all of these events contributed to where you are now in your life and how you feel about yourself?

7. In what ways does Lou's response remind you of your own experience of restlessness?

4
RESPONDING TO GOD'S LOVE: COMPASSIONATE SERVICE

This way has been tried, this way is certain.
—Fyodor Dostoevsky, *The Brothers Karamazov*

I. THE CENTRALITY OF SERVICE IN THE CHRISTIAN FAITH

What is the best possible way in which you can give yourself to someone else? How can you most fully, most richly give who and what you are to another so that he or she can receive your gift of yourself in a way that genuinely advances and furthers him or her? How, in other words, can you give yourself to someone else in such a way that your self-gift advantages that other and not, first and foremost, you?

To address this important question, let me direct your attention to one of the most startling claims in the New Testament. Indeed, I can not help but think that at least some of our earliest fellow-Christians must have been sorely tempted to say, "This is intolerable; it can't possibly be what Jesus meant. Let's simply omit it." The fact that the first generations of believers left it in is really quite astonishing and certainly very, very brave. The passage to which I am referring is Matthew 25:31–46, the familiar story of the separation of the sheep from the goats at the last judgment. The Son of Man will come in glory, and all the peoples of the world will be gathered before him. He will mount the throne of judgment and separate all humanity "as the shepherd separates sheep from goats" (Mt 25:32 NJB), putting the sheep on his right hand and the goats on his left. Then he will address those at the right: "Blest are you because when I was hungry, you gave me food; when I was thirsty, you gave me something to drink; when I was a stranger, you welcomed me; when I was naked, you clothed me; when I was sick, you visited me; when I was imprisoned, you came to me." And all those on his right will respond, "When did we ever see you in such straits? When did we ever serve you in these ways?" And he will reply, "When you did it to the least

50

of my brothers or sisters, you did it to me." And then he will turn to those at his left: "And you are condemned, because when you saw me hungry and thirsty, homeless and naked, sick and imprisoned, you did nothing for me." And they will object, "When did we ever see you in such a condition and turn away?" And he will tell them, "When you refused to serve the least of my brothers or sisters, you denied your service to me" (Mt 25:33–45).

To the best of my knowledge, this is the only passage in the whole of the collection of documents which we call the New Testament which describes the last judgment. The New Testament has a great deal about the end of the world or the end of this era of history, but there is not a syllable describing any criteria for the last judgment except Matthew 25:31–46. And notice what the only criterion of the last judgment is. There is not a word about whether you belonged to the church, not a word about whether you were baptized, not a syllable about whether you ever celebrated the eucharist, not a question about whether you prayed, nothing at all about what creed you professed or what you knew about doctrine or theology. Indeed, there is nothing specifically religious at all. Not one doctrine, not one specifically religious act of worship or ritual turns out to be relevant to the criterion for the last judgment. The only criterion for that final judgment, according to Matthew 25, is how you treated your brothers and sisters.

Now, it is startling enough that no explicitly religious belief or action is relevant to the last judgment. But it gets worse (or better, perhaps, depending upon your point of view). For notice, please, that *both* those on the right say to him, "When did we see you hungry, thirsty, homeless, naked, sick or imprisoned, and serve your needs?" *and* those on the left ask, "When did we see you in such need and ignore you?" One thing *both* the "sheep" *and* the "goats" agree on: they did not think about the Lord at all when they served or failed to serve their brothers and sisters. And both are told, "When you did or did not serve the least of my brothers and sisters, you served or failed to serve me." The astonishing point is that no religious motivation is the basis for the last judgment. Not only are specifically religious acts beside the point, so are specifically religious motives. The point is not that you love your brothers and sisters *for Jesus' sake*, but simply that you love your brothers and sisters. In effect, both sides reply to the Son of Man, "We didn't think about you when we acted—or failed to act—for our brothers and sisters. It wasn't for your sake." And in both cases the response is, in effect, "I don't care *why* you did or did not act; what matters is that you did or that you didn't."

Earlier in Matthew's gospel, Jesus has said, "Anyone who gives a cup of cold water to someone because he is my disciple will receive a reward"

(Mt 10:42). The story in Matthew 25:31–46 takes this a step further, maintaining, as it were, that anyone who gives another a cup of cold water *for any reason whatsoever* will be rewarded. The point is not that you serve your brothers and sisters for the love of God. The point is that you serve your brothers and sisters. What matters is not *why* you did it but *that* you did it.

In short, the ground for the final judgment is *agape*. The only relevant question at the judgment is, "Did you give yourself away to those who needed you?" That you did so because you are a Christian may be wonderful, but it is not significant for the question. That you did so because Jesus told you to do so, or because you cannot stand by and see someone starve, or because you simply enjoyed helping the other person, is all irrelevant. For whatever reason you did so has landed you on the side of the sheep. Once again, we come to the extraordinary Christian claim about *agape*. Whatever the motive, the issue is to give oneself away as completely, fully and richly as possible.

Of course, to say that the love of God is not necessarily the motive is not to say that the goal of giving oneself away is not intimately linked to our understanding of God. I simply mean that the link does not consist in God's being the explicit motive for our love of neighbor. Let me offer two images, both drawn from very perceptive nineteenth-century authors. The first is from Friedrich Nietzsche's *The Gay Science*, section 125, the section Nietzsche entitled "The Madman." This passage is famous because it is the first time that Nietzsche makes his famous—or infamous—proclamation that "God is dead." Section 125 is a kind of parable. A madman comes into the marketplace carrying a lantern and says that he is seeking God. The people who are in the marketplace laugh and ask whether God is lost. "Has he wandered off?" they respond, mockingly "Is he hiding? Has he emigrated?" But the madman turns on them and silences their sneers: "You do not know the great and terrible news. God is dead, and we have killed him, you and I. It was the mightiest deed ever done. We have murdered God." Those in the marketplace are thunderstruck when the madman presses his announcement further: "How could we do it? How did we erase the whole horizon? How did we disconnect the earth from the sun? Haven't you noticed that the world is becoming colder and darker, for the earth is spinning out into cold, empty space? There is no sense of direction now, no up or down, no forward or backward, no right or left." His hearers are shocked, and the madman sadly observes, "You do not realize your great and terrible deed! We have murdered God, and yet you do not realize what this means. We have to become bigger than we are to live within the cavity created by the death of God. We must become gods ourselves if we are to live in this world without God." And when the people remain in stunned silence, the madman leaves them, saying, "I have come too early. They are not yet ready to confront the consequences of their great deed—although they themselves have done it."

Nietzsche's parable suggests that the people to whom the madman speaks and who initially respond with ridicule have killed God and, in some odd way, already know that God is dead. But they cannot face that fact with all its immense consequences. I think that there can be little doubt that the madman and his proclamation are Nietzsche's depiction of himself and his work. He proclaimed to his age the news that his contemporaries knew but did not want to acknowledge fully, namely, that the idea of God which Judaism and Christianity had taught the western world and which had so deeply shaped the lives of men and women for centuries upon centuries in every aspect was now in fact dead. The people in the marketplace—the *laissez-faire* capitalist market-place of the nineteenth century, governed by social Darwinian, survival-of-the-fittest, dog-eat-dog competition—had killed the idea of God.

How could they maintain that the God who is least wrongly understood as pure and perfect *agape* is alive, and conduct their lives in the marketplace and increasingly outside it as though the deepest laws of life are "Always look out for number one" and "Do it to the other guy before he does it to you"? They might not want to accept the consequences of the way they lived, but they had in fact killed God, even if they still liked to use the word and invoke the idea. Nietzsche's immensely insightful and terribly uncomfortable point was that if the world of the nineteenth-century good, ordinary, middle-class, bourgeois Europe was the world in which one lived, then one lived in a world in which God is dead. Nietzsche, of course, thought that such a world was the only world in which one could live because it was the only world there is: a world indifferent to human concerns of love and happiness, hope and joy, justice and peace. But he also insisted that one could not delude oneself by dressing up that world with left-over notions taken from Christianity. One could not trot out God to comfort oneself when one was frightened or lonely. One could not go on appealing to the love of neighbor when such an idea only makes sense in a world which rests ultimately on the absolute agapic love of God, and God is dead. Instead, Nietzsche maintains, we must face the fact that we live in a universe which is indifferent to us and carve out a space for ourselves. We must become gods if we are to live without God. If we have eliminated God from our world, then we must live in a brand new way. What is that brand new way? We cannot be human any longer. Human beings need the reassurance and comfort of believing in God. If we are to live in a Godless world we must become superhuman. One has to be more than human to live in a world without God. Become the superhuman or you simply will not be able to live at all.

The second nineteenth-century image I suggest that we consider comes from Fyodor Dostoevsky. At the beginning of *The Brothers Karamazov* the youngest brother, Alyosha, is in a monastery where he has become a disciple of Father Zosima, an elderly monk who is a renowned spiritual director. Fairly early on in the novel Dostoevsky presents the reader with a series of brief interviews between Zosima and various people who consult him about their problems and questions. The series of interviews culminates in Zosima's conversation with a woman who says that she is deeply distraught, that she is uncertain whether she can live any longer with her life as it is. She tells the old monk that if he cannot help her, no one can, and she will have no recourse but to kill herself. Her problem is that she is terrified by her inability to believe in life after death. She cannot even dare to raise the question of believing in God. She does not know how she has ceased to believe. Once she did believe when she was a child, but now the world seems so dark, so cold, that she can believe in nothing, and her lack of belief is sapping every aspect of her life of its vitality and joy. Nothing in life seems to matter if there is no ultimate purpose, no final reason, no God. She can believe in nothing except, perhaps, the weeds that will grow on her grave.

Zosima tells her that what she is experiencing is the most terrible thing that a human being can experience, and that he thinks he can help her. He cannot offer her some abstract argument proving the existence of God, but he can offer her a concrete demonstration. What she must do is go home and every day, very concretely and practically, love the people with whom she comes in contact that day. If she does this, he tells her, she will gradually, step by step, discover that she believes in God. And should she approach truly selfless love—the *agape* of the gospel—she will find that she cannot *not* believe in God. Dostoevsky concluded by having Zosima tell the woman, "This way has been tried. This way is certain." And the rest of that long and glorious novel is, I think, an exploration of that claim.

Notice that Dostoevsky's woman without faith is very close to one of the people in Nietzsche's marketplace *after* the madman's announcement. She has come to recognize that in her world God is dead and she sees that the world is loosed from its moorings and becoming colder and darker. She knows that she cannot find her way up or down, forward or backward any longer, and she has discovered that she cannot live in this Godless world. But she also knows that she cannot go on pretending that she still believes in God simply because it consoles her. And Zosima tells her that if she is ever to believe in God she must first rediscover the people around her. Nietzsche's challenge is that if we live as if the law of life is selfishness, then whether we admit it or not, we do not believe in God. Dostoevsky's Zosima replies that if we wish to believe in God, we must live as if the law of life is *agape*. His advice is not "Go home and pray" or "Read the scriptures." Do not begin by thinking about God. Begin by loving those around you in the most concrete and practical ways. And then you will discover that belief in God is inevitable because the experience of God is so intimately bound up with the experience of self-gift.

We cannot experience God unless we love our brothers and sisters, and we cannot love our brothers and sisters without experiencing God. Dostoevsky is precisely right, I think. You cannot *not* believe in God if you truly love your brothers and sisters because you will experience your ability to love as being a gift to you, not of accomplishment by you. You will find yourself "doing" God, for God will be acting through you. Remember, God is more like a verb than a noun, not a lover but *love*. It is rather like someone asking, "Prove to me that there is such a phenomenon as breathing." It is not a matter of argument; the person is doing it! In a sense, the Christian demonstration of God is "I love you, therefore God exists." *Agapic* love is experienced as a gift not only by the one loved but also by the lover. For the carefully attentive and self-reflective lover knows that his or her love is so conditioned and so fragile that when it approaches true selflessness the lover's abilities are transcended. That transcending power which we encounter in loving another for the sake of the other is God.

II. DISCERNING OUR CALL TO SERVE

Ah, but how to give oneself away? How do we discover what our particular way of self-gift, our vocation, is? Or, to put it another way, how do we discern the will of God for us?

Before attempting to answer this question, there is a point of great importance to clarify about discerning God's will: to realize that God's will is not the will of some other person out there someplace with which we are supposed to bring our will into line. There is no all-wise, all-powerful person named God who has a plan for us and who gives us hints now and again what that plan is, hints which we are expected to decipher so that we can keep God happy by doing what God wants. That would obviously be a complete misunderstanding of what the Christian community means by God. God is not another person out there. And therefore the will of God is not a will out there. The will of God is the will within and beneath my will. The will of God is the will that carries my will. God's freedom allows me to be free. To find the will of God, don't look "out there"; drill down to the deepest depths of your own will, and there you will discover the will of God.

It is like looking at a great river. There are many, many currents on the river's surface. Sometimes it may even look as though the river is flowing backward upstream. But in fact, if you look at the river as a whole, it is always moving in one direction—from the mountains to the sea. The same thing is true of the will of God. The will of God is always moving in one direction toward one end. It is always self-gift. The will of God is *agape*, constant and perfect and eternal, and it bears all our wills with it. Sometimes our wills look as though they are going in exactly the opposite direction. But in fact, they are all being carried by that one great will. So, if you wish to discover the will of God, look to the depths of your own will. Discover what it is that you most really and deeply want when you are most really and truly you. When you are you at your best, what is it that you most truly desire? *There* the will of God is discovered.

There is also where the cross is found, because the cross is our desire to give ourselves away. It is our hunger to genuinely hand ourselves over, to give ourselves to others, because it is in doing so that we are most who we are. If you hold onto your life, you will not have life, but if you give it away, you cannot exhaust life. It becomes everlasting life. You become absolutely you. And who, finally, are you? You are the image and likeness of God. If God is pure self-gift, then self-gift is the image in which we are made, the blueprint on which we are built. Therefore, to give ourselves away is what we most deeply desire.

At times we may experience tension between our immediate situation, e.g. family obligations or the completion of studies, and our desire to serve. One of the most difficult lessons to learn is that one cannot do everything at one moment. Much depends on understanding the cycle in which we understand our lives. If everything has to be accomplished in twenty-four hours, then we must be impatient and attempt to perform the most important tasks immediately. But if we can live life in a seven day period, we can give ourselves a little more time for preparation for those all-important tasks. If one can plan one's life in month-long segments, then still greater long-range preparation can be given. And this is even more true, of course, if we can imagine our lives over the course of years. Service of others frequently demands both proximate and remote preparation. Remote preparation for service may be precisely what people may gain in the course of their university years, if those years are used well and wisely.

In St. Matthew's gospel there is an important instruction given by Jesus to his disciples when he sends them out to preach which does not appear in the gospels of Mark or Luke. You know the familiar story in which Jesus tells them not to take a walking staff or extra sandals or any money with them and to eat whatever is set before them. Basically Matthew includes the same instructions as we find in Luke. But Matthew adds one final instruction from Jesus: "What you receive as a gift, give as a gift" (Mt 10:8). This seems to me the ultimate instruction to all disciples: what you have been given as a gift, give to other people as a gift. This is why we must develop our talents. Why is your work at a university or for your family important? So that you can give it to other people later. There is a saying attributed to Catherine of Siena, one of the great women in the Dominican tradition, that the only reason to learn is to teach, the reason to gain knowledge is to give it away. What you receive as a gift, give as a gift.

But how do we find the best way to give ourselves away? What are some criteria that we can use in decision making? How do we discern our individual vocations? How do we discover what the call to service means for each one of us concretely? There are three signs which, taken together, are nearly infallible. The first is to discover whether this work or service is a source of joy for you. Please notice that I am again speaking of *joy*, not *happiness*. As mentioned in the previous chapter, happiness is dependent on a thousand external factors, whereas joy is the interior conviction that what one is doing is good even if it does not make one happy or content. Being happy cannot co-exist with being frightened or disappointed or lonely or dissatisfied or rejected, but being joyful can. Thus whether or not a particular way of living or working makes you feel happy is irrelevant to the discernment of vocation. But whether or not it is a source of joy, a profound conviction that it is a good way to live a life and spend one's energy and talent, is of immense significance. This echoes back to the discussion of restlessness as opposed to satisfaction. It is, in fact, the first sign that one may have found the will of God.

The second sign is ability and the opportunity for growth. Do you have the strength, the knowledge, the skills needed to live this life or do this work or serve in this way? There are really two questions intertwined here. 1) Do you have what is required for this way of living and working, and is that ability sufficiently formed and shaped at this point? If it requires more forming and shaping, more exercise and education, are you willing to undergo that training? 2) Will this way of living and working make you grow and continue to expand? Will it call forth your talents and gifts? Will it stretch you? This includes a willingness to confront reality, because reality makes us grow. Look for ways in which you pursue the truth of the matter, not what you wish for or what would make you feel good. If these questions can be answered affirmatively, then one may have the second sign of the will of God.

The third sign is that the vocation which you are considering is a concrete expression of *agape*. Does this way of living and working meet a genuine need in the community? Is it a real way to give yourself away to other people, not just something that you find enjoyable or challenging? Think about Matthew 25. In what ways can you most fully give who and what you are and have another person receive who and what you are in a way that genuinely advances that other person?

Notice that these questions, like those dealing with the second sign, can only be answered in community with others. The decision about joy is probably best dealt with in conversation with friends and a good spiritual director. But, finally, only you can answer "yes" or "no" to the question of whether this vocation is a source of joy. Both you and others must determine whether you have the necessary ability and whether others need you to serve them in this way. For others may not need to be served *in this way* or to be served in this way *by you*.

Now, take those three qualities together, joy, ability/growth, and *agape*. What is it that allows you to find those three qualities? Look for genuine joy, a genuine ability to affirm the rightness of being and the goodness of being creature, of being finite. Give genuine attention to reality, a genuine pursuit of the truth, built on your abilities. Look for ways that allow a genuine capacity to give yourself away. When those qualities come together, that is your decision. And that's the way in which, it seems to me, you discern your vocation.

No way of service is the only way or even the absolutely best way. You are not called to be Mother Teresa. *You* have to give *you*. You cannot give Mother Teresa for the simple reason that you are not she. You are a different person with different gifts and different abilities, with different weaknesses and different blindnesses. You have to discover what the best, richest, wisest way to give yourself is in your circumstances.

For example, for me the priesthood, the academic life and teaching are very important and fruitful ways that I can give myself in service to others. They provide wonderful channels for me to use what I think are most of my talents. Someone might say to me, "Why are you teaching? Why aren't you cooking in a soup kitchen?" My response would be, "Because I would be a lousy cook!" Certainly, cooking in that kitchen is neither more nor less important than what I am doing. But for me it is not as good a way to give myself away in service to others.

There is no absolute route to perfect holiness, no simple, universal rule. There is no absolute pattern except *agape*, and what *agape* requires in each circumstance, in each life, is very, very different. It may produce a Thomas Aquinas or a Dorothy Day, a Teresa of Avila or a Thomas More. It is astonishing to find all of the ways in which you, the unique and peculiar you, can give yourself away. That is why no one should simply follow another person's pattern for holiness. What one can and should do is take encouragement from others to find one's own pattern. There will be some ways in which you can model yourself on certain people and find common elements here and there. But you cannot and ought not become Francis of Assisi or Teresa of Avila, because if you did become Francis or Teresa, you would distort who you are. God has already given the world a Francis of Assisi. It does not need a second. Teresa of Avila did a splendid job of being Teresa of Avila. The world does not need a second, inadequate version. But the world has never had you and it does need you or God would not have made you, and so you have to discover the unique ways in which you can give yourself away in service to the world.

Another question to consider is: In what way do we work to change structures that are unjust as well as serve others? We have to capitalize on what is good in structures and we have to try to alleviate what is bad in them. Structures are neither as bad as we feel they are, nor ever as good as the people who made them think that they are. We could use the same basic statement of Augustine on restlessness as a way of dealing with structures: Even the best are going to be inadequate.

So there is a certain sense in which structures have to be accepted but at the same time criticized always. We have to allow the suffering of the poor to be the standard by which structures are criticized, that it's always the people who are most marginalized who will give us the perspective from which the underside can most clearly be seen. We have to respond on every level to the demands of the gospel and to the demands to enter into fellowship with all of our brothers and sisters. That is going to mean entering into fellowship on both personal levels and on communal levels. Unless we can work on both levels, we are not entering into full communion with the poor.

That means very clear-eyed, careful analysis of social structures, and, at the same time, recognition that after we have built the best of those structures, they are going to be inadequate. It also means that we cannot let go of personal engagement, never being allowed to simply retreat to the level of being the executive who decrees structural change, but is not personally involved in the building of those new structures. We have to work on both levels.

III. SERVING GOD IN THE
TANGLE OF OUR MINDS

The effort to discern how to give oneself away does not usually yield clear and irrefutable answers. Working through the discernment process is not like doing a mathematical equation in which you add so much joy plus an adequate amount of growth plus considerable *agape* and so arrive at one hundred percent. Seldom does one achieve that kind of clarity in life.

In his play about Thomas More, *A Man for All Seasons*, Robert Bolt has Thomas explain to his daughter Margaret why he is taking the difficult and dangerous position he does in opposition to the king. When she objects that she cannot understand how he can be so certain that he is right, More replies that he is by no means certain. But, he tells her, it is not his part to be certain. "God made the angels to show him splendor, as he made animals for innocence and plants for their simplicity. But Man he made to serve him wittily in the tangle of his mind!" That is, I think, precisely right. God does not want splendor or simplicity or innocence from us. God wants us to serve God in the tangle of our minds. Don't try to be an angel or, for that matter, a plant or an animal; be a human being. It is, in fact, much preferred to being an angel, let alone an animal or a plant. Isn't that, after all, the point of the incarnation? The one who is divine did not empty himself to become an angel but became human like all other human beings (Phil 2:6–7).

To be human is to be endlessly caught in a web of decisions among partial goods. It involves choosing between shades of grey, seldom if ever between absolute black and white. It means taking the risk of discerning the good and acting upon it insofar as you can see the good, knowing that you never see it with perfect clarity. To live and work and serve God and our brothers and sisters in the tangle of our minds demands infinite patience with ourselves and with one another. The most terrible thing that happens to people who are concerned about making moral decisions is that they kill other people who are concerned about making moral decisions but happen to make them differently. Remember, the inquisition was run by very good, really morally concerned people. If we realize that when we discern the good and make decisions, we do so in fear and trembling, knowing that we can never have full knowledge, perfect clarity, and final wisdom, then we may be less inclined to beat other people over the heads with the decisions that we have made. We must ceaselessly enter into conversations with others in the expectation that they too are trying to choose life rather than death (in the imagery of Deuteronomy 30:15), but, like us, are also puzzled about the various ways of moving toward life and away from death. And those varied paths must be honored and respected even as we criticize one another's choices, because we must begin by assuming that all of us are trying to serve God in the tangle of our minds.

One of the besetting problems of the church is the assumption that, somehow or other, faith leads to clear and simple answers. In my experience, faith seldom provides answers—but it does raise questions and prods us to explore the truth.

If, for example, you are confronted by a terrible tragedy—let us say, the death of a young spouse and parent from cancer—and you believe that we live in an essentially haphazard universe, then the death may be very sad, but it presents no great problem for one's fundamental attitudes toward life. But if you are confronted by that death and also try to maintain that the universe is in the hands of an all-good, all-wise and all-powerful God, *then* you have a problem. Faith is not the resolution of that problem; faith is what makes it a problem. There would be no difficulty if you were not a believer. Faith is what makes the tragedy into a real dilemma.

I suspect that we believers have to be more and more willing to share with one another and with others who are not believers that we live in the tangle of our minds. We must be willing to share with others the immense difficulty of trying to be authentically human in our world in our time. There is a strange and powerful image for this in Genesis 32:23–33. Jacob is returning to Canaan with his now quite large family after years away. He knows that he will have to meet his brother Esau, now a powerful chieftain, whom he cheated and who has no reason to love him. He cannot sleep and paces the river bank late at night. And during that long, lonely night he wrestles with someone. Neither he nor his assailant can prevail over the other, until dawn when the unknown adversary gives Jacob a sharp blow bruising his hip. But Jacob will not let go until his opponent blesses him. Then God—for he is, of course, the wrestling partner—renames Jacob Israel, which Genesis interprets as "the one who struggles with God."

To admit that our minds are in a tangle is to admit that all of us are engaged in fighting that midnight battle with God. Like Jacob, we have to fight all through the night, we must serve in the tangle of our minds, and know that we cannot get out of that tangle unscathed. It would be splendid to cut through that tangle, but splendor is for angels. Innocence would not notice the tangle, but that is for animals. And we are neither angels nor animals. We are human beings who claim the name of the new Israel, and so we are the people who struggle with God in the long and sometimes lonely nights. We are the people who struggle with God until we end up with a bruised hip, and it is that bruise which is the evidence that we have fought the good fight in the tangle of our minds.

For remember, the one undeniably true statement that we can make about God is that God is mystery. So we are people engaged in grappling with mystery, or perhaps better, people with whom mystery is grappling. The end of the story of Jacob's night of wrestling with God is that he left the Jordan bank limping because of his shattered hip (Gen 32:32). What a perfect image! Jacob goes limping across the Jordan into the promised land, and the limp is the proof that he has now become Israel, the one who struggles with God. The sign of being the true Israel is that you have been bruised in the struggle with mystery.

We must be willing to share the story of our limp with others by admitting in our teaching, in our relationships, in our service of others that we have not got a perfect and finished grasp of the truth but are eager to continue the struggle to clarify our partial vision. We may never find fully adequate answers, but the fight to find the answers is worth everything. For it is in the tangle of the mind that we become truly human and therefore also truly and authentically Christian. And the sign of that is that we approach the promised land limping.

In no aspect of our lives do we find our minds more tangled than when we grapple with the problem of evil. But everything we have said thus far is mere "whistling past the graveyard" unless we grapple with that mystery in Chapter 5.

Responses to Chapter 4

A group of four Notre Dame students met to discuss their reactions and connections to this chapter. These students refer to their participation in a variety of service experiences from which they find insight from Michael Himes.

Mike: The part of Father Himes' discussion of Dostoevsky that struck me was Father Zosima's advice to the woman who has confronted him with this rather engaging predicament. Father Zosima's advice is that you must go home and every day very concretely and practically set out to love those persons with whom you come into contact that day. If you do, bit by bit, you'll discover that you cannot "not" believe in God. This quotation speaks very clearly and specifically to my service experience which was to visit an elderly gentleman once a week for four months. What happened was we had a relationship that developed over a long period of time but did so in a very incremental way of forty-five minutes a week.

Student respondents to chapter 4 with Michael Himes (l to r) Sarah Keyes, Mike Barkasy, Katie Bergin and Bob Elmer

What I see is that I was able to plan what I wanted to do in the visits each week. But what happened when I got there each week was that I would be confronted with a situation in which I had to react in an instinctual way. What Father Himes said was you have to jump into it for the hell of it, which really struck me. At any rate, I found that I had to make adjustments in what I was doing.

The fellow I visited was quite a cook even though he was very physically handicapped and elderly. In his day, he was a great chef. Normally every week he would cook something for me. He cooked everything in the world. But one week he just decided he didn't want to cook and he was in one of his grouchy moods. Since he simply refused to cook, I took the leap of faith and asked him, "Well if you don't want to cook, maybe you could tell me what to do and I could try to cook for you." I really knew I was going out on a limb because this was really jumping into his turf. I wasn't quite sure how he would respond, and at first he was shaken by it. He wasn't quite sure how to handle it. Then he said, "Okay, let's give it a shot." So he gave me this huge recipe, from memory, of course, and we ended up throwing it together and it was just terrific.

I have difficulty putting into words the growth I experienced from that particular instance. What I felt was a real connection, something that I think goes back to what Father Himes said earlier, that God isn't really hovering over. God is not a distant being, but God is the relationship. God is the communication, right there, the actions that are involved in the relationship. That is what I felt in this situation.

Sarah: I was really struck by the same passage, particularly by Father Himes' explanation that we discover God when we love our neighbor because we begin to experience our love as a gift rather than as an accomplishment. We discover relationship, bit by bit, through small, concrete acts. If we don't experience our love as a gift, we find that it is inadequate. We discover a need for something greater.

Working this past summer at a homeless shelter for women and children made this idea hit home. When I first started at the shelter, I remember being conscious of everything I did, constantly analyzing my interactions, thinking through my every move. I wanted to have deep, meaningful conversations. I wanted to create powerful moments and build really intense friendships. But instead of feeling that I was getting anywhere, I remember feeling frustrated and inadequate.

Gradually, I realized and began to feel more comfortable and less self-conscious. I think that small, unexpected things began happening that made me realize I didn't need to think so big or try so hard. I remember one night in particular. At dinner, one of the kids spilled her Kool-Aid all over the floor. Her mother just shrugged it off and refilled the cup, even though she knew she was responsible for cleaning up the mess. I heard the woman mumble that she'd get to it when she was finished eating. But red, sticky footprints started to appear around the dining room, so I found a mop and handed it to her, asking her to clean the mess before it got bigger. I don't remember what I said to her, but I remember smiling and trying to make light of the situation, knowing that this is not what she wanted to do. She was an intimidating woman with a brusque manner, and I thought she might hassle me about it. But instead she grabbed the mop and stood up, rolling her eyes and laughing. She shook her head as she laughed and said, "Sarah, I like you." Surprised, I just laughed with her.

That woman didn't stay at the shelter much longer. I don't remember talking with her at length again, certainly not in a long heart-to-heart conversation. But something was shared between us. I don't know when, or understand how, but we had indeed formed a relationship. When I left the shelter and looked back over the summer, I realized that many more relationships, even friendships, had snuck up on me. It had all been beyond my control, beyond even my awareness. It was not something I had created or accomplished, but a gift that had been given to me.

Bob: I really like the idea of needing to find joy in the service that I do. I think of my experience in Appalachia, which involved working on homes, helping build, paint and various other kinds of manual labor. I did not find the manual labor enjoyable. I think some people might find it enjoyable in and of itself, but I didn't *until* I met the people whose homes we were fixing. When it was just a building, I would work on it a while, but then I could get frustrated and want to give up. When I met Annie, the woman who owned the house we were working on, and was able to share with her, then the work became a joyful experience.

When she came outside and was a part of the group, although she never actually picked up any tools, I enjoyed working with her and for her. I could then look at the house and not just say I accomplished painting it, but that I helped this person experience some of the joy Father Himes describes. So in a way similar to what Mike and Sarah discussed, I find joy in the personal contact. For me, it is the relationship part of the service that I think Father Himes is talking about when he says that we have to find joy in what we do and only then will we be of service to others.

Katie: Father Himes says that experience is the ground for theological reflection. After listening to Mike, Sarah and Bob, I realize that they confirm this idea. I too can more easily see a concrete relation between service and God when I think, consider and discuss my experiences. For example, a significant story from my summer comes partly from my memory, but also from writing about the encounter.

I was in Hawaii, working with people who have leprosy. One day, Hymen asked me if I would like to drive over to the other side of the peninsula to Kalawao, where the original settlement of leprosy patients were sent (*forcibly*). He picked me up promptly at dawn and began almost immediately to narrate his life story. He had had six hours of surgery on his arms with no anesthesia—an illegal operation done on him because he was not human. He was a *leper*. He showed me the scars on his body and his words showed me the scars on his heart. I listened and cried. I looked and tried to understand.

Out about a mile in the ocean are two land formations—small islands that dot the rough and tumultuous sea. "There," he said, "is where the ships used to stop and dump people in the ocean because they were afraid what would happen if they got too close to this contagious spot called Kalawao, Molokai. They estimate over a thousand died in the water trying to swim to shore." Standing on the land, you can see nothing but graveyards now. Unmarked graves as well. "You are stepping on holy ground. Do you see the bones? Do you sense the Spirit here?"

And in the blowing sea air, I felt strangely drawn into the love of God. Standing in the midst of death, I felt a sweet summons to life. Hymen opened his cooler and had carefully prepared mango chunks for me, the *haole* (white girl) who loved mangoes so much. How could love prevail in this land marked for hate? How could a eucharist be shared between an old man and a young woman when death awaited? The Spirit in the air was one of peace and painful memories. This Spirit whips through this deserted peninsula and touches all who stand there. You can just sense something present. In the simple act of shared mangoes, Hymen and I were swept up into this love best known and least wrongly named as God.

In discovering the best way to give myself away through agapic love, a journal of past attempts can be insightful! Holding together both action and reflection is helpful in my discernment process. I find it important to share with others the struggles and questions which exist in "the tangle of our minds." Entering a conversation about compassionate service, for example, with Father Himes, a few friends and people like Dostoevsky, Catherine of Siena, Francis of Assisi, Dorothy Day and Teresa of Avila can be extremely interesting and not a bad way to spend an afternoon!

Questions

1. Read Matthew's gospel (25:31–46). In your own words, write what you believe to be the meaning of the text. How does it apply to your life? to the life of your faith community?

2. Do you believe with Nietzsche that "God is dead"? Why or why not? Give three examples which support your point of view.

3. What is a vocation? What is an avocation? In your experience, which gives you greater joy? Interview three other people and compare the results.

4. How is it that the cross is found wherever the heart's desire is found?

5. With regard to your own situation, ask yourself the three questions which test the authenticity of one's service or vocation. Share your responses with one other person.

6. What is faith? How does faith assist the believer in times of struggle?

Journal Questions

7. Apply Zosima's advice to yourself. For seven days love every person with whom you come in contact concretely and practically. Record your experiences daily and after seven days write about your experience of God through others.

8. What is it that lies at the very core of your being, that which you must do, which makes you happier than anything else? Write whatever comes to mind, in whatever order it comes to mind. Take a walk, or leave it for a few hours. Reread what you have written, then reflect on the way in which God's will is aligned with yours.

9. Share with one other person an experience of struggle, either with God or in another relationship such as the service relationships described by the students. Ask the other person to do the same. Later, write what it felt like to share this with another person. What did it feel like to hear your friend's story? How important is the sharing of stories in our lives?

5
VULNERABILITY: SUFFERING THE MYSTERY

One Crucifixion is recorded—only—
How many be
Is not affirmed of Mathematics—
Or History—

—Emily Dickinson

I have a quarrel with the way in which chapter 3 of Genesis is often understood. Frequently sin is described as though it were rooted in pride. I think that this is a fundamental misreading of the implications of the story. Maybe the clearest revelation of how much of a misunderstanding it is has been demonstrated by Milton. Anyone who has read *Paradise Lost* will remember that the character which the reader finds most interesting, most exciting, and perhaps even—were truth told—most sympathetic is Satan. Adam and Eve are given some magnificent poetry, to be sure. Various of the angels have splendid speeches assigned them, and God has some fine passages. But there can be little question that the most memorable, most often quoted, and most dramatic poetry goes to Satan. Indeed, considering that all the action in the story depends on Satan, it is very hard to avoid construing Milton's great epic in such a way that Satan becomes the protagonist. Why? Ultimately, I think, because Milton sets out to make Satan a monster of pride. But the problem is that pride is a failing that Satan shares with most of the great tragic heroes in our literary history. The fact is that, monster of pride though he may be, Milton's Satan is a fairly close cousin to Othello or Lear and a brother to Achilles and Hector. When he thunders that it is "Better to reign in hell, than serve in heaven" (1:263)—although Milton clearly hoped that his readers would murmur, "Bad, bad, bad"—I suspect that most readers have felt a secret thrill, and perhaps so did Milton himself.

This hint of a tragic hero about Milton's Satan stems from the fact that pride is not the depth of evil or the root of all sin. At least it is not what we find in Genesis 3. The great Hebraic insight into sin is that the essence of evil is despair and that the self-assertion which may appear as pride in fact springs from despair.

To cite another great poet, Dante got it right. In the *Divine Comedy*, the entry to hell has inscribed over it, "Abandon all hope, you who enter here" (*Inferno* 3:9). The gateway to damnation is the abandonment of hope, despair. And when Virgil finally leads Dante to the very lowest circle of hell, he finds Satan locked in ice made of his own tears frozen by the endless beating of his wings vainly attempting to rise (34:28–54). And Satan says nothing. Imprisoned in ice, endlessly weeping—this is no monster of pride. This is a monster of despair; despair leads one into hell and despair is the deepest pit of hell. Far from being the assertion of one's own absolute value, sin comes from the inability to believe in the value of anything.

The most chilling—and, I think, accurate—statement about evil that I have ever read comes from Goethe (to introduce yet a third great poet). In the First Part of *Faust*, when Faust first summons up the demon Mephistopheles, he demands to know, "Who are you?" Mephistopheles responds with two answers, both of which are immensely insightful, but the second chills to the bone. First, he replies that he is "A part of that power that forever wills evil and forever does good" (ll. 1335–1336). When Faust dismisses this as a riddle, Mephistopheles then tells him, "I am the spirit who forever says 'No'! And rightly so, for all things that are, come to an end. Better there should never have been anything" (ll. 1338–1341). In regard to the spirit who says "No!" I cannot imagine that Goethe did not have in mind St. Paul, who tells us that in Christ there is not yes and no, there is only yes (2 Cor 1:19). By contrast, in Mephistopheles there is only no. No to what? No to everything. Is there any ground for hope? No! Any possibility of growth? No! Any reason to go on? No! Is there any value to you? No! To me? No! Is there any point to anything? No! The spirit who says "No," the spirit who denies, the spirit who insists that everything is junk. Why is it all junk? Because "all things that are, come to an end," all things are finite. Everything is limited, and, therefore, "Better there should never have been anything." It is all trash. Better it all be done away with—including Mephistopheles.

You see, only one thing is worthy of being, according to that demonic claim: God. Be God or be nothing. Only God deserves to exist, and if I am not God and you are not God, then we are trash and ought not to be. Evil is the endless willing of non-being. Mephistopheles, the demon, is the antithesis of Jonathan Edwards' definition of "true virtue," the consent of being to being; he is the being who absolutely denies being. Better there be nothing.

The antithesis of this is, of course, the divine willing of being. Not only does God bring all things into being by willing them, Genesis insists, but God has declared that creatures, the same finite beings which Goethe's demon deems unworthy of existence, are good (Gen 1:4, 10, 12, 18, 21, 25, and 31). The Christian response to evil must be the affirmation of the goodness of finite being. So we are all engaged in affirming and fulfilling our being, not denying it. And that fulfilling of our being is our capacity for self-gift, as we have discussed in Chapter 4.

But there is an enormous difficulty in trying to talk about the problem of evil. If ever we think we have answered it, then we have made evil less than evil. Every answer to the problem of evil is necessarily wrong. Let me give an example. Imagine that I am teaching a class of pre-med students in a course on physiology and that I have assigned as a term project the construction of a model of the human body to include the skeletal, vascular and muscular systems and all the organs. On the day assigned, you produce the model, and after examining it, I ask you what the small space next to the liver is. You reply that it is space for a tumor. Well, of course, there are sometimes tumors on some people's livers, but we would not expect to build space for such tumors into a model of the human body. Indeed, once you build into such a model of the body some room for tumors, you make the tumor something normal, something to be expected. You are implicitly justifying its being there. But the tumor is what should not be there. And that is the problem in trying to answer the question, "Why evil?" Evil is, by definition, what should not be. So if you construct a system of the universe that adequately explains why evil exists within it, you have justified it, and then it is no longer evil. Evil is always that which cannot be finally explained because it is what ought not to be. Its being is self-contradictory.

Indeed, remember the first answer Mephistopheles gives when Faust asks who he is: "A part of that power that forever wills evil and forever does good." Faust ignores this response as a riddle, but it is really a profoundly insightful statement. Goethe's point is that the demon, the embodiment of evil, forever wills non-being but by the very act of willing affirms the fact of its own existence. It cannot help but use the power of its own being, its will, to deny its own being. It forever wills evil, i.e. chooses non-being, but forever does good, i.e. implicitly affirms and exercises its own being. Evil is literally absurd, self-contradictory, self-frustrating, rather like someone insisting at the top of his lungs that he is not there.

Thus we must recognize that there is no satisfactory answer to the problem of evil. In fact, if one were to find any answer fully satisfactory, it would be a certain indication that it is wrong. So we have to acknowledge that we will remain dissatisfied with whatever response we give to the questions, "Why evil?" "Why suffering?" "Where is God in all this?" But that is no reason not to say something in response to the questions. We must remember that whatever we say will be something, but not everything and never enough.

In trying to say something, we must discuss two issues which are bound to confront people who set out to serve others: first, what are God's role and our role in responding to people's suffering; and second, what difference does our belief in the crucified Christ make as we try to fathom "hopeless" situations of suffering?

I. GOD'S ROLE AND OUR ROLE
IN RESPONSE TO SUFFERING

One of the most dangerous phrases that religious believers toss about with abandon is "the will of God." Often it is used as a way of dismissing the full impact of the pain and suffering which surround us. "Submission to the will of God" offered as an answer is not only remarkably ineffective as a consolation to ourselves or to others (to whom it is more often offered), but it also verges on blasphemy. For it seems to imply (if so unmeaning a response can imply anything) that somehow or other the pain or loss at issue is willed by God or, in a less directly offensive form, permitted by God. Directly or indirectly, this places the burden of responsibility for the world's suffering on God's shoulders. Then, of course the question becomes why God does not do something about it. No one has phrased the problem better than the American poet Archibald MacLeish in the jingle which runs through his verse play, *J.B.*: "If God is God He is not good,/ If God is good He is not God." Attempts to dodge the issue by distinguishing between the "active" and "permissive" wills of God are simply that: dodges. Once again it puts us in the position of nattering on about God's will (or wills) as though we have a perfect grasp of absolute mystery. Indeed, as has been said earlier, the Christian tradition maintains that there is one least wrong way to speak about God, and therefore about what God wills, and that is as pure *agape*. From the perspective of that fundamental Christian metaphor for God, the will of God is simple—it is self-giving love.

An initial way of responding to the question of why God does not do something about the world's pain is to say that God has: God created us. If we have chosen either to increase that pain or to shirk the responsibility of dealing with it, then we have little reason to talk about that pain as the will of God. It may more properly be ascribed to our will than God's. Our task is to discover what the *agapic* will of God and our call to be *agapic* mean in confronting our and others' suffering. But if we have not creatively, imaginatively and courageously allowed that love to find expression, to ask "What's wrong with God?" rather misses the point. We refuse the responsibility of the vocation for which we are made and to which we are called and then blame the one who made us and gave us the vocation.

Genesis 3, the Adam and Eve story, insists squarely that evil with its attendant suffering and destruction enters the world as our doing, not God's. But then the question arises why God made us capable of choosing evil. Should God not have created us as able only to love? God made us capable of being like God which means capable of self-giving love. When we read that God has made us in God's image, if the fundamental Christian metaphor in 1 John 4:8 and 16 is right, we are the image of *agapic* love. We are created as a result of the divine self-gift to be self-gift. But if we are created capable of *agape*, and if *agape* is free or not *agape* at all, then we must be created free. If we are created free, then we also have the capability of denying what we are. And that is precisely what the Christian tradition understands as the origin of evil—the denial of the very depths of our own being. It may be absurd, self-contradictory, self-frustrating, but that is what evil is.

We are created because we are loved and in order to love, and we say, "No, we are not lovable and we shall not love." Why did God make us capable of refusing to love? Because if God had made us capable of loving and incapable of not loving, then our love would not be *agape*. *Agape*, self-giving love, is by definition free. I suppose one could say that the whole of creation is an enormous divine risk: God so loves us that God creates us to be what God is, running the risk that we will blow the whole thing. But if that risk were not run, we could not be what God is because we would not be free. And there is the entry-point of evil. Evil is the refusal to be what in fact we are, the denial of our being good, the denial of our being loved, the refusal to love ourselves or others. So some evil does come from us, but as the misuse of our freedom, not as a necessary result of its use. Instead of loving freely, we freely decide not to love. Evil is the complete twisting of the gift of freedom.

Everything that God made God has declared good. We tend to say that being human, indeed, being finite, i.e. being creatures, is not good. We have looked at creation and declared it a mess. In all sorts of ways, like Mephistopheles, we have decided that it would be better if it had never been. Where then does the intense suffering, the destruction and loss which we see in our world come from? At least in part, the answer seems to be that it arises from our disdain for and misuse of the world.

Let me give an example. Every few years, it seems, Bangladesh suffers terrible damage as a result of monsoons. Our newspapers and television screens tell us of the immense loss of life, the terrible destruction, the enormous grief of the people of Bangladesh who have seen their families, their homes, their crops and animals swept away in catastrophic storms and floods. One might well ask, "How does God permit this suffering? Why does God send these monsoons year after year?" But if the monsoons do not come, central India experiences massive drought and thousands of people may die as the result of famine. So is the monsoon an evil? If you happen to live in central India, you might think it a great good. But it is experienced as an evil if you live in its path in Bangladesh. Now, who decides that hundreds of thousands of people will live on low-lying land in the path of the monsoons, facing the dangers of horrendously destructive floods year after year? Who decides how land is distributed in the third world countries of Asia—God or we? The evil is not the monsoon, the evil is that people must live in its path. God does not force them to live there; we human beings are the ones who have made that decision. If one drives the Titanic onto an iceberg, one should have the decency not to exclaim, "How terrible of God to create icebergs!"

People die—that is part of being finite. That people die in terrible pain, alone, uncared for, without dignity—that is evil. How much money will be spent in our country, in all the countries of the world, this year on armaments? If all that money, all that energy, all those resources, all that planning, all that technological skill were devoted to research on, let us say, cancer instead of arms, would so many people die in so much pain and perhaps at such young ages? And who votes on the expenditure and allotment of money and resources? God or us?

My point is that we too easily ask, "Why is God doing (or permitting) this?" when God may more justly ask, "Why are they doing (or permitting) this?" Too often we look at the conditions of finitude which we have distorted and made hideously painful and degrading and ask, "Why has God done this?" God made us free in order to love. If we invert that freedom and reject that love, whose responsibility is it—God's or ours? Too often when we talk about the problem of evil and suffering we end by saying, implicitly if not explicitly, that God should not have created us free, which is to say that God should not have created us human. But that is tantamount to saying that God should never have created us in the first place. And somewhere in the background, if you listen closely, you will hear the voice of "the spirit who forever says 'No!'" muttering, "Better there should never have been anything."

There is a subtle temptation here for all who try to commit themselves to serve others. The experience of suffering, dark and meaningless suffering can all too easily provide us with reasons to choose not to participate consciously in the world around us, a world filled with lonely and hurting people. So, for example, you give a great deal of time and energy to trying to be present to someone who is alone, ill, aged, dying. And the person never responds, never seems to grow through the relationship which you have tried to establish with him or her, never appears to appreciate the love which you offer. Let us say the person dies, and your efforts at service have made no apparent difference whatsoever. The temptation will be very strong to conclude that the effort was not worthwhile, perhaps that the effort was foolish, a stupid thing to have done, something which it would be better never to have done. Is there not a vague whiff of the Mephistophelian about such a response? The whole business was a waste of time, better it should never have been. Yes, he or she died. My efforts come to nothing. Everyone and everything comes to an end. Nothing is ultimately of value.

The most devastating effect of evil, rooted as it is in despair at creatureliness, is that it drains goodness, beauty and power from everything. The evil we may have to confront in trying to serve others in *agapic* love is not only that which we find in the suffering of others but that which we meet in our own discouragement and frustration before the reality of pain and death. And one way this finds expression is the abandonment of our creative response to evil in the world and the lapse into anger, resentment or resignation before the question, "Why doesn't God do something about this?"

In Genesis 1:26–27 we read that we are created in the image and likeness of God. At that point in Genesis, what do we know about God? To that point in the story, what have we seen God doing? Creating. So if we are fashioned in the image and likeness of God, we may conclude that we have been made to be creative. Thus we should not think of the world in which we find ourselves as finished before we are placed in it. The universe is still being created, and we are called to create it along with God.

But if that is true, then we cannot begin by asking why there is disorder and chaos and suffering in the universe, as though we were dealing with a finished product of which we are simply the consumers. We are called to work with God in creating order out of chaos. When we confront the enormous problem of pain in our world, we must recognize that God has created us as co-creators who are supposed to be working with God to relieve suffering and grief.

So, when you are immersed in attempting to assist others in pain—physical, spiritual or psychological—where is God? God is to be found in what happens between you and the others. But God is not simply present in and under your self-gift to those who are suffering. God is overcoming the evil of their suffering How? By undergoing it. That is the deep wisdom of the symbol of the cross in the Christian tradition. Death is overcome by dying. God does not overcome evil by a simple snap of the divine fingers. Any such ideas reduce Christian faith to magic. The only way in which death can be overcome is by undergoing it and embracing it within something bigger and more powerful than it. The suffering which we experience through our own lives and the lives of people around us is overcome by its embrace.

II. JESUS AND THE CROSS

Within the Christian tradition, we claim that there is one particular point in our experience, in our world, in our history, where everything that we mean by God is embodied, absolutely displayed before us, completely present to us. In the life, death, and destiny of Jesus of Nazareth we see in human terms what it means to be God.

So a very great deal obviously depends on what we say about Jesus of Nazareth. And if what I shall now say does not shock you, then you have thought long and wisely about what we ought to say about Jesus. We may feel uncomfortable saying what is clearly the truth about Jesus of Nazareth: he was a monumental failure. Indeed, the whole point of the gospel is that Jesus of Nazareth failed. The gospels do not tell the story of someone who succeeds in his mission. Rather, they are the story of one who undertook an immense task and failed.

The gospel tells of one who came to proclaim the kingdom of God is upon us. Have you noticed the kingdom recently? Have you bumped into it lately? Nineteen centuries later and there is not a great deal of evidence that Jesus was right. He proclaimed that the meek would inherit the earth. And has anyone noticed *that* happening? Jesus announced that peacemakers would be called the children of God. More often they are called busybodies and pests. He promised that those who hunger and thirst for justice would be satisfied. Oh? He informed us that those who are sorrowful would be consoled. Really? All sorrow gone? The fact is that again and again we find that the message he proclaimed does not seem to have worked. Jesus selected a group of twelve close associates. One betrayed him, one repeatedly denied him, and the others ran away when he was arrested. He ended by being excommunicated by his religious tradition and executed as a criminal by his government. He died by public torture and was buried in someone else's grave. Not a whopping success by any standard.

The striking image of the cross no longer hits us with its full force. We have tamed it into a religious symbol and have lost its shocking, scandalous quality. The cross is an instrument of torture. What an astonishing thing that a religious community should take as its primary symbol an instrument for torturing people to death. It would be like a religious community today choosing as its chief symbol a gallows or an electric chair or a gas chamber. Our principal symbol for the absolute love and power of God is a means of execution—and that tells you much about Jesus as a failure. For the Christian claim is that God is not the one who comes into the world and conquers it; rather God is the one who comes into the world and loses everything, even his life. When the fullness of the presence of God enters our world, it is rejected, people do not listen to it, and it ends by being thrown out by religious leaders and dispatched by law. What an extraordinary claim about the presence of God! Where is God found? Not with those who win, but with those who lose.

Out of the massive defeat of Good Friday, lo and behold, God brings something totally new, a destiny more glorious than could have been imagined before the catastrophe. Unless we grasp how utter a disaster Good Friday is we cannot appreciate how overwhelming the triumph of Easter is. And the symbol of the victory is an empty tomb. Life comes where you have no right to expect it. It does not come from success. It is found among those who seem to lose everything.

The cross does answer the question, "How can God will (or permit) this suffering?" and the answer is that God does not will or permit it. God hates human suffering. God will not tolerate the pain of God's creatures. Then, given the terrible reality of suffering in the world, where is God to be found? God suffers with us. God does not permit the cross, God is on the cross. By dying, God overcomes death. By suffering God defeats suffering. That is the point of the Christian claim about the death and rising of the Lord.

God is not "out there" somewhere watching human beings suffer here and letting it happen for some "higher" purpose of God's. God is here suffering with human beings. God does not will suffering; God does not permit suffering. God's will is mysterious only because it is so simple. God wills love. Period. God wills love, all the time, and that is all God wills. So suffering is not an obstacle to the presence of God, suffering is one manifestation of the presence of God.

There is a very odd element in the passion narrative in John's gospel. When the crowd arrives to arrest Jesus in the garden, Jesus asks them, "Whom do you seek?" They reply, "Jesus of Nazareth," and he tells them, "I am he." The gospel of John then says that the crowd withdrew several feet and fell to the ground, unable to rise (Jn 18:4–5). Only when the question and answer are repeated are they able to get up and seize Jesus.

The fourth gospel seems to be using an image from Psalm 27:2 which says that the wicked who come against God's chosen will stumble and fall.

But why bother to make the point at all? It is, I suggest, a very strong way of claiming something which is also implied in the synoptic gospels: the cross is not something that happens to Jesus, it is what Jesus has been aiming at all along. Luke's gospel reports that "when the time drew near for him to be taken up, Jesus resolutely set his face for Jerusalem" (Lk 9:51). All the synoptic gospels agree that Jesus repeatedly told his disciples beforehand that he was going up to Jerusalem to be betrayed and tortured and executed but that he would be raised up on the third day (Mt 16:21; 17:22; 20:17–19; Mk 8:31; 9:30–32; 10:32–34; Lk 9:22; 9:45; 18:31–33). The insistence is that the cross is not a catastrophe which happens to Jesus. The cross is the goal toward which Jesus advances. John's gospel insists on this so strongly that not only is Jesus depicted as being in sovereign control throughout the passion but those who seek to arrest him cannot even seize him without his permission. Earlier in the fourth gospel Jesus had said that he lays down his life in order to take it up again (Jn 10:17). Clearly, it is Jesus who is laying down his life, not others who are taking it from him.

For Jesus, the cross was in some way the object of his desire. It was not something that was given to him, but something for which he reached out. How can that be? The answer is found in what is the most often repeated statement attributed to Jesus in the synoptic gospels. It appears in various guises, the wording changes slightly, but the basic form of the saying remains constant: the one who holds onto life loses it; the one who gives life away sees it become everlasting life (Mt 10:39; 16:25; Mk 8:35; Lk 9:24; 17:33). That statement is, in fact, the key to the whole gospel story. For a long time when I heard or read that line, I interpreted it as a commandment. Only gradually did it occur to me that it is not a commandment but a description. Jesus is not telling us, "This is how you ought to live," but rather, "This is how the world is. This is what it is like to exist." If you give your life away, it becomes everlasting life, but if you hold onto it, you lose it.

This is obviously true if one begins from the claim that God is perfect self-gift. If the very source and ground of being, God, is self-gift, then it follows that if you really want to be human, give yourself away. To the extent that you choose not to give yourself away, to that extent you do not fully exist. If I am correct in understanding this fundamental claim as a description, and if it is a true description, then the gospel is a parable about someone who tells parables. It is a parable to demonstrate the truth of the claim that existence is proportional to self-gift. The Gospel is the story of one who does indeed give himself away totally to the will of his Father and to the service of his brothers and sisters. He gives himself away so totally that he comes to the point that there is nothing left to give: "Father, into your hands, I give my spirit" (Lk 23:46). "All that I am, the very breath of my being, the very center of my existence, I now give to you, Father." And so, "It is finished" (Jn 19:30). What is finished? Jesus is finished. There is nothing left, like a sponge which is wrung out. Jesus gives himself away completely, and because there is nothing left to give, he cannot not exist. The tomb cannot hold him. If you give your life away, you will see it become everlasting life—that is precisely what we claim about the death and resurrection of the Lord: having given himself away perfectly, he lives absolutely. He lives now to die no more.

If that is so, then the cross as the symbol of the ultimate act of self-gift is precisely the great goal of Jesus' life. To borrow a phrase from John Dunne, CSC, it is Jesus' "heart's desire." And so the gospels insist, in the deepest sense, Jesus has chosen it. It is not imposed on him. "No one takes my life from me, I lay it down freely, and as I have power to lay it down, so I have power to take it up again" (Jn 10:18). It is Jesus who comes to the cross, not the cross which comes to Jesus. This transforms the understanding of the cross in Christian life.

At the moment of death Jesus is most clearly himself and therefore most clearly the revelation of who God is, which is why the fourth gospel can insist, "When I am lifted up from the earth, I will draw all things to myself" (Jn 12:32). This is the reason why his death is the hour when the Son of Man is glorified and the Father is glorified in him (Jn 13:31; 17:1); it is when Jesus is most clearly, most perfectly who he is. And so we come to see the cross as the point toward which we are all advancing by our own deepest desire, if only we knew it. It is what we really want most deeply, if we could ever know what we really want. It is for the cross that our hearts are restless, in Augustine's language. The cross is the symbol of our desire to give ourselves away. It is our hunger finally and fully to hand ourselves over, to give ourselves to others, because it is in doing so that we are truly who we are. If you hold on to your life, you will not have any life, but if you give your life away, you cannot exhaust your life. It becomes everlasting life. You become absolutely you. And who, finally, are you? You are the image and likeness of God who is pure self-gift, the blueprint on which we are built. And so to give ourselves away is what we most deeply desire. But if the whole Christian life centers about self-gift— and I think it does—then why am I bothering to write this? And perhaps more to the point for you, why are you bothering to read it? Why aren't you out of your chair and off to serve your brothers and sisters? What has theologizing got to do with agape? Well, before you dash off to love the first neighbor you bump into, look at the next chapter.

Broken and Blessed
RESPONSE BY REG WEISSERT

I have done quite a bit of writing in my life, but never have I gone through the agonizing exercise of writing on the topic of suffering. I have reflected often on the suffering I have seen in the slums of Manila and Venezuela, in the *poblacions* of Chile and the *pueblo jovenes* of Peru. Even though they were remote, I could see how the suffering in those places happened because of greed and power and money. I came away from each of these exposures resolved to do something about my own lifestyle and to translate those remote situations to the problems of poverty in my own country and city. Here were the examples of evil that Michael Himes talks about in this chapter.

When I reflected on what Michael had to say, I thought of two aspects of his theme. First of all, the vulnerability. The people I talked to and walked with in these other places lived in destitution and were *vulnerable* to the political, economic and social structures of the world—evil structures—that "which should not be," in Michael's words. The blame could be laid not on God but upon structures and people who allowed and participated in perpetuating the poverty, hunger, and the lack of education, medical attention, housing and beauty. I knew that I, too, was guilty when I did not raise my voice in defense of the voiceless or use whatever influence I had on their behalf.

One of these people who represented for me so many others was a woman named Sylvia. She was babysitter, housekeeper and friend to my daughter, Susan, in Lima, Peru. Sylvia had come from the mountains with her family, looking for a better life in the city. As so many people from the countryside did, she wound up in one of the slums—*pueblo jovenes*—that surround this dusty, arid city of Lima where people live without sanitation and intermittent water and electricity. Her husband left her with five sons to raise, and the only thing she could do was domestic work. Every day she came by bus from miles away, came to watch another's child and clean another's house. On each visit of mine, I saw Sylvia. Since my Spanish was minimal and because Sylvia spoke a hybrid Spanish mixed with Quechua, her native dialect, I relied on my five year old granddaughter to translate. But I found language no barrier, for here was another woman and mother, caring about the same things I did but living a far different life, a life she had no control over.

On my last visit, Sylvia was noticeably sad and cried several times. She seemed forgetful and complained that her head hurt, but she refused to stay home. She was afraid of doctors and hospitals and was convinced she

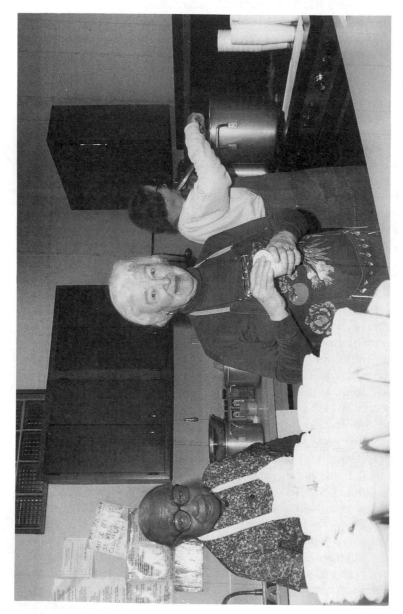

Reg Weissert (center) with volunteers at St. Augustine's soup kitchen

was going to die, an idea we tried to talk her out of. One afternoon we drove her home to her little house and once again she wept because she was so poor and we saw her poverty. When I left Lima she gave me a little gift—a cheap, glossy ceramic piece with the words "con amor" (with love). That little gift sits on my dresser so that Sylvia is always remembered. Her intuition had been so right. Two weeks after I returned home, Sylvia died of a brain tumor. I think of Sylvia's vulnerability and that of thousands of people like her condemned to lives of poverty by the evils of the world—that which "should not be." The evil is that so many people are at the mercy of those who have power—the power for good or the power for evil. The evils are correctable but the correction must be done by those in power. I think, too, that Sylvia always lived with hope. Despite her suffering she never despaired but believed that, somehow, God would come to her rescue.

The second part of Michael's title "Suffering the Mystery" is more difficult to deal with. We try to understand and explain suffering that does not directly touch us. I wish Michael had developed that idea at greater length—the aspect of personal suffering—for it seems that in our own personal suffering the question of "why" cannot be answered. So often, there is no one to blame—God, society, the doctor, one's self (although the temptation is always there to do that), external evil. It just is.

My greatest personal loss was that of my husband, friend, lover, companion, of forty-two years. His death so suddenly and unexpectedly left me with that big question "why"—why, when there were so many other people inching toward death with terminal illnesses? Nothing made sense. Since there is no answer to the "why" the only alternative is acceptance and faith. The closest Michael comes to answering the question is when he states "The suffering which we experience through-out our lives and the lives of people around us is overcome by its embrace." This is a hard saying because, rather than "embrace" suffering, we flee from it. It is more acceptance than embrace. When I was younger, I tended to put difficult situations of any kind out of my mind and not think too much about them. Maybe if I didn't think about a problem, it would go away. Wishful thinking, of course, for it doesn't go away but lurks in the background, demanding resolution.

As I've grown older, my answering to this mystery of suffering is to put it in a faith dimension. If Jesus is our model for life, then we must see his life in totality, not only how we must love, but how we must suffer and die. His own acceptance is the best example we have—the mystery.

I was struck with Michael's assertion that Jesus was a "monumental failure." I like to think that He was a success. How can we explain, otherwise, that for two thousand years people have followed his message, both the educated and the illiterate, the poor and the wealthy, the losers and winners, those who hope and those who despair. His success is in that message of love and service that is both profound and simple. His love led him to the cross, and, as Christians, we see how in our "cross" his love is there to sustain and console us. Suffering is a mystery—but so is our God.

Questions

1. Define evil in your own words and give three examples of evil from events in the news.

2. What is the cause of so much suffering in the world? How do we reconcile suffering with a good and gracious God?

3. Review Chapter 1 and our discussion of agapic love. What is the relationship between agapic love and the cross for all believers? Give an example of this relationship.

Journal Question

4. Reflect on the passion of Christ in the gospel of either Matthew or Luke. After reading it, pray the events of the passion with the following excerpt in mind: "Death is overcome by dying. The only way in which death can be overcome is by undergoing it and embracing it within something bigger and more powerful than it. The suffering we experience through our own lives and the lives of people around us is overcome by its embrace." (p. 74) What meaning does this quote take on for you? Can you relate the events of the passion to an experience of struggle and perhaps death in your own life? Does Reg Weissert's response help you to make connection between the passion of Christ and your own suffering?

6
CONVERSING ABOUT
THE MYSTERY

We have no theology. We dance.
 –*Hirai*, quoted by Mircea Eliade, *No Souvenirs*

I. THEOLOGY: THAT OF WHICH
WE CANNOT SPEAK

There is a charming story which I have heard told by both Mircea Eliade and Joseph Campbell, two of the most prominent students of comparative religions in this century. Both have included it in their writings. At a meeting of scholars of the history of religions held in Tokyo in the 1950s, the participants were escorted to many of the major Shinto shrines and witnessed a number of impressive Shinto religious ceremonies and celebrations. Toward the end of the conference a distinguished western sociologist found himself in conversation with an equally distinguished Shinto priest named Hirai. The sociologist remarked that he had been enormously impressed by the beauty and solemnity of the Shinto ceremonies. But, he said, he could not quite understand what the participants thought they were doing in the ceremonies. Could the Shinto priest explain the meaning of the actions. "What," he asked, "is the theology behind these celebrations?" Hirai listened respectfully, thought a moment, and replied, "We have no theology. We dance."

I suspect that there are some very committed Christians who would say, if asked, that they have no theology, they just act for others. There is no question that Christianity is, first of all, a way of life, a call to self-gift, and that the creed, the system of Christian doctrine, follows from that way of life. And so sometimes people who generously respond to the call to Christian service have little patience with theological reflection. Theology, they think, is all well and good for those who like that sort of thing, but we have more important things to do. We must be about actively loving our neighbors. And they are right—except that I do not think that one can truly serve one's neighbor and not be engaged in critical reflection on the experience, reflection which can only be called "theology."

Theology means "talking about God." But that presents an obvious problem: How do you talk about absolute mystery? How do you talk about that which by definition you cannot talk about?

Earlier in this century, Ludwig Wittgenstein, the very influential philosopher, concluded his *Tractatus Logico-philosophicus* with a famous proposition: "Of that about which we can say nothing, let us be silent." Wittgenstein was leaving room for what he later described as the mystical. And before mystery he held that silence was the only possible response. Once you have reached the point at which language fails, stop talking. Do not go nattering on as though you know what you are talking about when, by the very definition of mystery, you don't.

Of that about which we cannot say anything, let us be silent. That is an immensely important injunction in theology. Theologians must constantly remind themselves that they are skating on very thin ice over infinitely deep ponds. No one ever knows the depth of what he or she says about God. All language about or to God—including creeds and doctrines and forms of prayer—is, by definition, inadequate. So, one might well conclude, why not follow Wittgenstein's maxim and be silent?

Certainly, Wittgenstein's famous proposition is one of the boundary lines within which theology is carried on. But there is another boundary line which I think has been given fine form by T.S. Eliot (who was, in fact, speaking of poetry although I think the remark applies aptly to theology): "There are some things about which nothing can be said and before which we dare not keep silent." Some things, we know, cannot be said adequately, but they are so important, so central to our lives, that we cannot possibly not try to talk about them.

An example occurs to me of something that has to be said even though we all know that our words will be inadequate. In his film "Manhattan," Woody Allen has a scene in which he tries to tell a young woman, played by Mariel Hemmingway, that he loves her. He works up his courage to the point that he blurts out, "I love you." But then he immediately says, "No, no, no, I don't 'love you.' *I love* you. No, no, no, no, no, I don't *love* you, I llllove you. No, no, no, I loooove you. No, no, no, I lovvvve you. No, no, no...." And he tries one way after another to say those three words. The point, of course, is that the words do not adequately say what he means. The phrase has become so hackneyed that the three words do not mean anything anymore. "I love you" simply does not say what we experience about our attraction and devotion to this other person. Indeed, no words do. It cannot be said. But, with all due respect to Wittgenstein, we cannot be silent about our feelings for this other person. We have to try to say what we mean and feel, even though we know in advance that we will fail. Eliot is right. Some things are so important that, although we know that we cannot say them adequately, we dare not keep silent. We must keep trying to say them.

For example, think about a wedding when a man and a woman stand publicly before their families and friends to say to one other, "I take you as my companion for the rest of my life." Those words mean a lot more than the couple can possibly understand or imagine at that moment. No one at the moment of the exchange of wedding vows knows what those words will mean five years down the line, let alone twenty-five or thirty-five years. But would it be wiser to counsel the young couple, "Since you cannot know what these words will really mean, since you cannot possibly understand all the depth and breadth of their implications, simply remain silent: say nothing"? Of course not. The words demand to be said, although all the people at the wedding, including the bride and groom, know that they do not really know what the words of the vows will mean. It is another moment when we skate on very thin ice over very deep ponds—like prayer and theology.

It is between these two poles, that noted by Wittgenstein and that given expression by Eliot, that all theology is carried on. The theologian has to keep constantly in mind that he or she does not know how to make his or her words adequately express absolute mystery. After all, the theologian is talking about what is ultimately significant about existence. But on the other hand, the fact that the theologian does not know the full depth of what he or she is attempting to articulate does not mean that he or she can simply abandon the attempt to say it. God is simply too important to us not to talk about. We are in the position of always talking about what we know we can never say fully.

Many people engaged in the work of serving their brothers and sisters may very well ask, "What has this to do with me?" After all, they may say, they are not theologians. And that is true, *if* by theologians one means someone who has a graduate degree in theology and teaches the subject. But remember, theology means "conversing about God." And I maintain that you cannot talk about your experience of serving others without talking about God—sometimes without knowing that you are.

I find that one of the most difficult things for people to understand about theology is that almost everyone has a theology already. After all, if I say the word "God," you don't turn to the person next to you and ask, "What was that? How do you spell it?" Something goes on in your head when you hear the word "God." Whatever that something is, is a reflection of your theology. Now, your theology may be good or bad,

critical or uncritical, traditional or untraditional. It may be very sophisticated or very naive, but it is theology. What happens in your mind or
your imagination when you hear the word "God" is incipient theology.

So neither I nor anyone else needs to supply you with a theology; you
have one. What may need to be done is to assist you to bring your
theology into conversation with many other people's theologies to see
whether it is more or less adequate and to determine whether what you
think about God fits with all the other things you think and do. The
question of the "fit" between your idea of God and all the other aspects
of your life is crucial. To answer it you do not need to get a degree in
theology (although that is no bad thing to do). But you do have to think
critically about theology.

If we do not think about theology, we may far too easily end up in a
sort of intellectual schizophrenia. We can erect water-tight bulkheads
between one part of our minds and our experience—the part of our lives
when we pray, read scripture, go to church, talk about God—and all the
other parts of our minds and experience—the parts when we consider
how to make a living, choose an occupation, decide whom to marry,
raise our children, spend our money, vote, deal with our next-door
neighbors, etc. All those kinds of questions become secular issues,
having nothing to do with what we think about God, which is, after all,
what we think about the ultimate mystery which undergirds all that
exists. Not only does this impoverish our thinking about most of the
concerns of life, but sealing "God" off in a separate part of our minds
inevitably renders our belief in God unreal because it is unconnected
with reality. If thinking about God is to be real at all, then it has to affect
and be affected by all the aspects of our lives. If the word "God" means
anything at all and especially if "God" means what the Christian
tradition claims, then how we live as human beings shifts radically.

There is no way in which someone can responsibly say, "Ah, yes, the
God-issue is an interesting question, but I shall bracket it for the
moment." One might as well bracket breathing for the moment in order
to attend to other things. The question of God cannot be bracketed as
one question, however important, among many others. It is an aspect of
every question one asks about one's life. Thinking critically about
theology is terribly, terribly, important.

So, are you engaged in theology? Of course you are. Every time you
ask a question like "Why should I get out of bed this morning?" you are
dealing with what is ultimately a theological issue. Getting out of bed or
pulling the covers over one's head because you cannot face the world is a
statement about the meaning of life, about your standard of good and
evil, of right and wrong, of value or worthlessness. One might name that

standard in different ways; one name for it is God. You are involved with thinking about God all the time. You may avoid it. Of course, you may not always be engaged in thinking about some "supreme being" out there in the great beyond. But, then, that has nothing to do with what we as Christian believers mean by "God." Even atheism is a kind of theology. After all, to say that God does not exist means that you have some meaning attached to the word "God" and that you have decided that the meaning is not realized in fact. Even that is a form of talking about God, of theology.

II. THEOLOGY: REFLECTION ON EXPERIENCE

Theology is not a process of applying in various situations, personal and social, certain doctrines for which we claim some kind of special status because Jesus revealed them or they are in the Bible or the church teaches them. Were that the case, theology would be at best an imposition on experience and at worst utterly irrelevant to it. But if we understand theology as a reflection on the deepest roots of all human experience in order to see how all experience relates to our being believers, then theology and experience become very relevant to one another, indeed.

But why should we reflect theologically on experience? Theology does not immediately seem to be relevant to all experience—for example, to our experience of being in relationships. You may be engaged in conversation with friends and God is never mentioned in the course of your talk. What then is the theological significance of that conversation? The answer, of course, depends on what you mean by "God." Were God the supreme being out there someplace, then God could be at most a third party who listens in on the conversation. But if God is least wrongly thought of as the relationship of pure and perfect self-gift, then I suggest to you that an experience of true conversation with others is the experience of God. God need not be the topic of the conversation. God is the ground of the possibility of there being a conversation. You are engaged with God and God with you quite apart from the topic of the conversation. Wherever there is genuine self-gift, sharing of self, giving of self to the other, there is the experience of God. God is never a third party to the conversation; God is what happens in the conversation.

Theology is the attempt to give the right name, the deepest and truest name to what is going on. The reason to talk about God in the experience of relationships is not that we are arbitrarily importing something from the outside into the experience but that we discover something in the relationship itself.

Let me explain how I think you may discover this most directly. In my experience when one genuinely loves *agapically*, that is to say when one loves the other person for the other person's sake, not primarily for what one gets from the relationship, one's spontaneous response to the discovery of one's ability to love in such a way, if one is careful and honest in discerning it, is gratitude. We find ourselves grateful for being able to love other people. We experience the capacity to love other people *agapically* as something given to us, not something we produce. Our ability to give ourselves to others is itself a gift to us, not some kind of self-affirmation, not an exercise that we perform, but a gift given through us. To demonstrate this all I can do is to invite you carefully and perceptively to examine your own response on those occasions when you catch yourself genuinely loving agapically. I think you will discover that your immediate reflex response is "Thank you." And the "you" in that "thank you" is what we mean by God.

The experience of genuine *agapic* love is joy in the other person's existence, not for any good which that person's existence can do you, but simply because he or she *is*. This is an example: I have a niece and nephew, and I admit to being a doting uncle. For me the whole universe is justified by the fact that Elizabeth and Andrew exist. That the dinosaurs died out, that the crusades were fought, that Columbus sailed, that human beings have walked on the moon—it is all right so long as the universe finally produces Elizabeth and Andrew. And when I reflect on the experience of joy in their existence, I find that I am grateful not only that they exist but that I can love someone in such a way. And gratitude is the immediate response to the experience because the ability to love in such a way is recognized spontaneously as a gift given to us, a capacity which we are permitted to exercise. That is why we have to use the language of God; we have no other language to describe this experience of transcendence. The capacity to rejoice in the being of the other as the other is not adequately described in my experience by language which roots the capacity in me; it requires language for an experience given to me and through me. That is why we end up using theological language when we talk about loving others.

It is possible that someone may feel awkward using theological language. It is, after all, a technical language. But it is also a language that many women and men over the course of the centuries have found powerful and descriptive because they have found that what they have experienced is named by theology. For you see, theology does not arise out of other people's experience first and foremost, even other people in our religious history. Our concern with theology is not how well it describes the experience of Abraham and Sarah and Moses and Mary and Jesus. Our concern is how well theological language describes our experience. Does the Christian theological description of God and the world name your experience? To be sure, other people's experience may be immensely illuminating and expansive of our experience, which is why the experience of Abraham and Sarah and Moses and Mary and Jesus remains of great importance within the Christian tradition. Indeed, it is why there is a Christian *tradition* in the first place. But you must not try to wrench your experience around to match up with someone else's. Examine your experience and ask, "Does the Christian theological tradition describe what I find to be the case?" "Does it challenge me to rethink my understandings?"

III. REFLECTION ON SERVICE EXPERIENCE

I fear that we sometimes play off service and reflection against one another, as if to question our experience critically is in some way to sap it of its vitality. That is an immense mistake. One cannot, even with the best intentions and deepest concern for one's neighbor, plunge into any action of service without recognizing that critical questions need to be asked about the situation: What is really needed, how did the need arise, what means are available for responding, what resources does one have for dealing with it, what resources does the gospel provide for one's response? And at the same time, I must critically reflect on why I am concerned about my neighbor's need in the first place: Is it making me feel better about myself, is it assuaging some guilt, is my response a covert exercise of power? To assume that we can brush such questions aside and move directly into action is as immense a mistake as thinking that all we need do is analyze the neighbor's situation and not act to meet his or her need. Reflection and action must be held in tension with one another.

The self-giving love which leads us to act to serve others should also motivate us to address the critical questions: What is really needed in this situation and what is the real basis for my involvement? Like everything else about *agapic* love, this is not easy; some will try to avoid acting by simply asking the questions, and some will immerse themselves in their action and never face the questions. But unless reflection and action are held together, no truly effective service will be given (except, possibly, by accident) and no real growth will occur. The deepest reason for this is that we are called *as full human beings* to serve others. Human beings have hearts and heads, *and* both must be brought to self-gift. To act as though one need only be led by the promptings of the heart is to decapitate oneself. The head has been left out.

Of course, to assume that all one need do is understand a situation for it to be remedied is to fall prey to the great platonic mistake that all evils are errors, so if the error is understood the evil will disappear. Alas, the fact is that it is perfectly possible to know what the truth is or what the good is and still not embrace it. That is what we mean by sin. And sin is never reducible to a mistake in judgment. We cannot intellectualize evil and suffering. Nor can we trust to our desire to love, for neither the heart nor the head is immune to sin.

One way to understand the need for both action and reflection is to think about the relationship between religion and theology. Religion is the name for a way of life and action; theology is a name for reflection on the ground, meaning and goal of that way of life and action. John Henry Newman suggested that theology stands to religion as criticism stands to art. If I may elaborate his point, after you read all the best critics on *Hamlet*, you still need to see the play; after you are led through detailed analysis of a Mozart piano concerto, you have not replaced hearing the concerto. The work of art is richer than anything anyone can say about it. But that does not make the work of literary or musical criticism unnecessary or fruitless. The more you know about a poem or a piece of music or a painting, the more deeply, richly and fully you are able to enter into the poem or piece of music or painting. Criticism presupposes the work of art and never replaces it, but the work of art is enriched by the appreciation of the wise and perceptive critic. Newman is, I think, quite right: the same relationship holds between living the Christian life and doing theology. Theology is not a replacement for living religiously, by any means. But theology can serve living the Christian life by enabling us to understand what the depth and breadth of living the Christian life actually demands, to see its roots and its implications. Theology never replaces service. It enriches our service so that we live lives of service in a more fully human way.

The great American philosopher William James used to tell his students at Harvard in the first decade of the twentieth century that life is bigger than thinking about life: you do not live to think, you think to live. And the same thing is true about theology and Christian service: you do not live the Christian life to understand it; you understand in order to live it more fully.

IV. DEEPENING ONE'S RELATIONSHIP
WITH GOD THROUGH SERVICE

In the first letter of John we read, "Anyone who says 'I love God' and does not love his brother is lying, for whoever does not love the brother whom he can see cannot love God whom he does not see" (1 Jn 4:20). Such a person is not necessarily a liar in the sense of one who deliberately falsifies the truth, but he or she is one who abuses the truth in that such a person does not know what he or she is talking about. If you claim to love God whom you do not see but do not love the brother or sister whom you do see, you quite literally do not know what you are talking about, because you do not know what the word God means.

The author of the first letter of John is not talking about God as an idea, or the conclusion to an argument or the end of a long and complicated proof. He is talking about God as a part of our experience, "something we have heard and seen with our own eyes and watched carefully and touched with our own hands" (1 Jn 1:1). He is talking about God as one might talk about one's friend, i.e. as part of one's experience. For God is part of our experience. Notice that the author of the first letter of John does not ask us to believe in God; he asks us to recognize that we have encountered God with our own ears and eyes and hands.

And where do we encounter God? According to the first letter of John, we encounter God as the ground of our capacity for loving others—and also of their capacity for loving us. Wherever we experience—in ourselves or in others—a deep, intimate and loving relationship, there is our primary experience of God. Remember: *ubi caritas et amor Deus ibi est*—wherever there is charity and love, there is God. The deeper and clearer our reflection on our relationships of self-gift, the more our humanity is engaged and so the more richly we experience our encounter with God. And the richer our encounter with God, the richer and more fully *agapic* the relationship with others. Each feeds the other.

Were one to say, "In my service I find no need to talk about God at all," I think I would have to ask the questions, "How deep is your relationship with those you seek to serve? How completely does it embrace your full humanity?" Think for a moment about one of the most basic and most demanding of relationships: genuine conversation. I do not mean chit-chat to pass the time of day. I mean real conversation, which demands conversion on the part of the participants. First, I have to attend to what you say to me, to understand what you mean and how you mean it, to switch sides and put myself in your position, as it were. Then, having tried to incorporate what you see and think and feel, I have to try to convey to you what I see and think and feel and to do so in a way that will be comprehensible to you. Meanwhile, you are making the effort to understand what I mean and how I mean it. You are switching sides and putting yourself in my position. Then, having attended to me, you must try to incorporate what I have tried to say and then attempt to respond to it. And I am once again trying to move to your side of the table, to see the matter as you perceive it. No wonder genuine conversation is so exhausting! And no wonder we do it so seldom. "Conversation" is very intimately related to "conversion," and "communication" to "communion." I have to give myself to you as well as I can, through my words, my gestures, my tone of voice, to make myself, my mind and my heart, available to you. And you must strive to receive that gift as fully as possible, to see what I see, hear what I hear, and feel what I feel. And then we reverse roles.

This is a tremendously draining process! It is a miracle that anyone ever does it! Precisely it is a kind of miracle, an act of mutual transcendence. And I do not think that there is any true service of others, any genuine self-gift, where that attempt at conversation, at stepping into the other's place and seeing the world through the other's eyes, is lacking. Without it service becomes a pleasant stroking of our own egos, a disguised form of vanity. Nor do I think we can describe that transcendence without, implicitly or explicitly, using God-language, i.e. theology.

The separation of theology and agapic service of others is a variant of what I have come to think is the single most pressing ethical problem in the Christian life, holding together truth and love. I think that virtually every ethical issue that we confront in every area of our lives is in some way a variant of this one great problem. We must never separate truth and love. Never sacrifice the truth to what you think is love of the neighbor. There is no real love in disguising reality from someone because we fear that it will hurt him or her or because we worry that he or she will be unable to deal with it. Never sacrifice loving your neighbor to what you think is the proclamation of the truth. The truth is falsified when "we call it as we see it and let the chips fall where they may," when we forget that truth is itself relational and is found equally in the ear of the hearer and the mouth of the speaker and so must be said in a way, at a time, in a place that makes it possible for the hearer really to hear it. The great moral achievement is to speak the truth lovingly and to love truthfully. It is not enough to seek the truth or to act in love. We are called to do the truth in love. In trying to reflect on our experience theologically, the Catholic strand of the Christian tradition furnishes no more fruitful and insightful notion than "sacrament." Indeed, I maintain that what makes Catholicism catholic is its sacramental vision. In the following chapter we must talk about that vision.

*Andrea Smith Shappell (left) and Don McNeill, C.S.C. (middle right) with
students Katie Glynn and Christopher Fahey*

The Search for Understanding: Methods of Reflecting on Experience

RESPONSE BY DON MCNEILL, C.S.C.
AND ANDREA SMITH SHAPPELL

In our personal experience we have found that theological reflection has been most pressing in times of the loss of a loved one, and in times of service to others. Both of our mothers suffered long illnesses before their deaths. In the process of being with them through their struggle we found much of what we teach about caring and compassion, aging and dying open for questioning again.

From our own conversations with men and women, in the present and the past, who have explored their faith in relationship to "the depths of our human experience," we find new insight for our own journeys and to bring back to the classroom. What we continue to present to students are ways to make the connections between their experience and the insights of theologians.

In our experience of discussing Michael Himes' presentations and material in small group, educational settings, we have found that the insight of Michael's that many latch onto is Matthew 25 (Chapter 4)—it does not matter what motivates us to serve as long as we do it. We would often jump in at this point with the question to Michael, "Why, then, do you see that it is important for us to do theology?" Certainly it is attractive to many to continue the dance of serving others without reflecting on what the meaning of the actions are. Many struggle to make a connection between theology and experience. Therefore, we feel that Michael's reflections in this chapter are essential to the whole of the book.

We invite others we work with in group settings to see that theology is not a separate part of life but, as Michael states, "a reflection on the deepest roots of all human experience." We use a variety of ways to help group members link theology and experience, all of which are methods appropriate in a variety of settings. In addition to a structured reflection in secondary and higher education, these methods work well with parish groups like RCIA, hospice workers, and outreach ministry groups reflecting directly on service.

We present below a few methods and examples of linking faith and action followed by an example of theological reflection on experience.

1. Journal Writing: A frequent criticism by those who resist writing journal reflections on their service experience is that they remark, in the same strain as Wittgenstein, that words cannot express the depth of their experience. Our response is that the journal is the place to attempt to express that which is difficult to put into words. Journals can be read by a spiritual director, parish minister, or religious educator to point out and help name the experience from a theological perspective. The following example from Christopher Fahey's journal raises questions of suffering, presence, compassion and creatureliness which were later pursued in dialogue with the Himes readings. Christopher was a student visiting an eighty-five year-old man named Frank in a nursing home.

Visit 5

Frank admitted to me today that he was scared. Apparently his right foot began tingling much like his left foot had before it had to be partially amputated. He said it felt fine but I still worried for his sake. We talked more about his wife who died a few years ago as well. Every once in a while, he slipped into the present tense. Perhaps it makes him feel good when he remembers his wife and all they have been through. I liked seeing Frank happy. It made me feel as if I was helping him through this painful part in his life. Suddenly, his mood changed.

Choked up with emotion, he said, "I try and say a prayer in the morning just to help me get through the day—sometimes it works, sometimes it doesn't."

I saw that there still was a lot of unresolved pain within Frank. I only hope that my presence will comfort him in his struggle. Just as quickly as it had changed before, his mood changed again. We talked about the Olympics for a while and I then asked him if he liked it here. To my surprise, he answered that he thought that he had had a positive experience here. I didn't realize that Frank had such a positive attitude toward being in the home. At the end of the visit, he told me that he would say a prayer for me and I told him I would say one for him.

2. Reflection Questions: Specific questions can help name the theological concepts and insights from the readings or videos, such as those of Himes, and ask for connections to one's experience. In this example, Bridget Spann responds to a question about the use of the terms "the less fortunate" and compassion. She explored the biblical underpinnings of the word "fortunate" and then connected it to a reading from *Compassion* (by Nouwen, McNeill, Morrison). She also related these insights to her own experiences.

In no way is compassion a reaching out from on high to those who are less fortunate below. First of all the term "less fortunate" is problematic; on a materialistic level, we imagine ourselves to be more fortunate because of the many possessions we have. Sometimes one's economic status perverts a person's perception of what is necessary for the good life.

Compassion, as defined in the introduction of *Compassion*, connotes suffering with another. To be compassionate we are called "to unmask the illusion of our competitive selfhood" and "to give up clinging to our imaginary distinctions as sources of identity" (20). This radical challenge cannot be met if we allow our envisioned "good fortune" to separate us from others. In seeking to be compassionate we must follow the self-emptying example of Christ:

> His state was divine, yet he did not cling to his equality with God but emptied himself to assume the condition of a slave, and became as we are; and being as we are, he was humbler yet, even to accepting death, death on a cross (Phil 2:6–8).

Compassion, a movement of solidarity in recognition of our common human brokenness, must involve a conversion of our heart, and not of our wallets.

The term "less fortunate" has negative and false implications. Fortune in some ways reduces life to a material level. It is easy to misinterpret the events of relationships in another's life as unfortunate. The reality of the situation is that we can never know, except when the person permits us to share in his or her suffering.

Now I recall Mitchell, a "less fortunate and underprivileged" man who contends that being HIV+ is the best thing that has ever happened to him. It stopped him in his tracks, and forced him to evaluate the content of his life. Since then Mitchell makes time for the truly important things in life while experiencing a faith never before realized. If anything, Mitchell had compassion for me, someone who has not yet completely accepted my death in order to really start living.

The questions at the end of each chapter invite you to engage in this type of theological reflection.

3. Role Plays: Enacting particular service encounters helps to raise questions and to prepare one for anticipated difficult situations. A role play involves the two or more persons in the encounter and at least one observer of the interaction. After the situation is acted out both participants and observers comment on the interaction.

An example of this is the importance of ritual which helps to express the meaning of a significant relationship when saying goodbye. Through a role play, one may better identify what he or she wants to say to the other about the meaning of their time together and also to think of an appropriate symbol which helps to express what is not easily said. Himes refers to the added dimension of this kind of relationship: this is an experience of agapic love which "is not adequately described in my experience by language which roots the capacity in me; it requires language for an experience given to me and through me."

When the theological naming of the experience cannot be shared with the other person in a service relationship, a ritual may express dimensions of the mystery which cannot be verbally shared. Whether the ritual is an embrace, a picture of those in the relationship, or a small gift, it symbolizes what the relationship means. And from this understanding of ritual in a relationship, what connections can then be made with the meaning of religious rituals such as eucharist? Thus, the role play can lead to further discussion and journal reflections.

4. Conversation: As Michael points out, conversation is intimately related to conversion. Through the conversation in the service relationships and through the small group discussions, conversion often begins. Sometimes the conversion is a small step of deepening the understanding of God in one's life. Other times conversion throws one into questioning one's faith, future plans, lifestyle, etc. What we see here is that this is a lifelong process of conversing and being open to conversion.

Katie Russell describes her deepened understanding of what it means to serve others after reading and discussing Himes' insights on Matthew 25:

> Service to others, whether in simple, daily ways with family and friends, or in more dramatic forms, such as the summer service project, becomes ever more significant to my faith and myself. Himes' explanation of Matthew 25 bluntly reinforces the meaning of my interaction with others for my faith: "Love your brothers and sisters because that's how you love God" is often a difficult and uncomfortable challenge.
>
> On one hand, Himes' reflection may seem liberating and easy as it de-emphasizes the rules and rituals of the church which are sometimes difficult to understand or relate to. Conversely, however, the ramifications of truly loving our brothers and sisters are immensely challenging and life-altering. To give ourselves away to one another completely is not an easy or trivial accomplishment. The extent of such a love is tremendous. It does not come without discomfort, inconvenience, and effort. I am not called to serve my brothers and sisters only on Mondays and Wednesdays from 4:30 to 6:30 at the Homeless Center. It is not enough to love only the people I like. I cannot give of myself only when I have extra time, resources, or energy.
>
> To truly love and do for others, in whatever manner, requires faith and the help of God. Though serving and loving others may sometimes be a natural human reaction, to be selfish and irresponsible is just as human. Serving others, reacting to their needs—action which comes out of real love—often requires discipline. Real love and service is not simply a "knee-

jerk reaction." Genuine love of others requires the strength to be motivated to make yourself disciplined, the courage to delve into the lives of others despite their positive or negative reactions, and the faith to believe that you are capable of service (that you are worthy enough to have something to give).

5. Searching and Restless Questioning: We encourage all learners to continue questioning with the spirit of Himes' chapter on restlessness. Katie Glynn's reflection provides an example of restless searching:

Two years ago I visited El Mozote, a village in El Salvador and the victim of a brutal attack in 1981 by the El Salvadoran government. Suspecting that the villagers were FMLN sympathizers, the army was sent to massacre them. The men of El Mozote went into hiding when they received word of the attack, assuming their families would be unharmed if they weren't there. When the men returned, however, they found their wives, children, and grandparents dead—murdered by the El Salvadoran army. The economic, political, and social situation of El Salvador, something I had "prepared" myself for through readings and videos, did not prepare me for the human faces the village of El Mozote represented.

When I returned to the U.S., I felt helpless in the face of such injustices and had no hope that the world would ever change. How do I integrate what I saw, felt, heard? How do I make sense of the contradictions of this world and of my life? How do I live so that others may live justly? How do I take action? What action should I take? How do I help to change the evil institutions that dictate our world? Where do I start? I desperately wanted answers to these questions. I wanted a way to combine the two worlds of which I was now a part.

I struggled with how I could be in solidarity with the people of Latin America while I was living in the United States. Can I say that I am in solidarity with these people when I have never known what it is like to be without food, water, a house, to be tortured, or live in war? Can I say that I am in solidarity even though I will never know what it is like to be a non-white, oppressed, or a poverty-stricken Mexican or Salvadoran?

I still have not arrived at the point where I can forgive the soldiers, the governments, the churches, and myself for the role we have played, and continue to play, in the violence done to our innocent brothers and sisters. But I no longer look to the Catholic Church, the United States, humanity, or God for answers to these questions or reasons for this inexcusable violence. Instead, I thrive on the questions. I live for more questions.

I have had to set out on an unmarked path to create a way of life consistent with what I believe. I have had to redefine my search. The search for answers—for stability, for security in institutions—has been replaced by the search for questions. I have had to learn how to live with questions, and how to regard the struggles as gifts. Another question represents a new possibility, another alternative for a new way of living in this world. Any answer that could be given to me now would come from this world, from the experiences of this world. Questions, however, do not come from this world. They come from the restless search to create another world—a world of peace and love. When the questions end, when the restlessness ends, the hope dies. As long as the questions remain, there is hope left for the people of this world to finish the creation that God began.

Our attempt is to invite students and others into the lifelong struggle of holding together truth and love, theology and agapic service. It is the stories of those in the present time and throughout the ages who live this struggle that challenge us to **do the truth in love**.

Questions

1. What does "theology" mean? How is every person involved in "doing theology" all the time? Give examples.

2. What is the difference between theology and religion? Explain how Newman understands the differences.

3. What is meant by gratitude? How does Father Himes describe gratitude? Give examples.

4. What is the "great ethical dilemma" of this age? Do you agree or disagree? Why?

Journal Questions

5. What is "doing the truth in love?" How is your own life a manifestation of doing the truth in love?

6. What methods of theological reflection are most helpful to you? Give an example of linking theology and your experience.

7
SACRAMENTAL VISION

These things, these things were here and but the beholder/Wanting.
      –*Gerard Manley Hopkins*, "Hurrahing in Harvest"

I. THE WORD

The most important Catholic theologian of the twentieth century, Karl
Rahner, held that words are the operative element in sacraments. To
understand what he meant, there is a possible misunderstanding which
must be ruled out. The words do not refer to the actual formula spoken
in the course of the sacramental celebration. So, when in baptism, while
pouring the water over the person being baptized, the minister of the
sacrament says, "I baptize you in the name of the Father and of the Son
and of the Holy Spirit," or when in the eucharist the presider says the
words of consecration over the bread and wine, "This is my body. This is
the cup of my blood," these formulas are not what Rahner meant by the
sacramental word. Indeed, treating those formulas as the operative
element of the sacraments would reduce sacraments to magic—as long as
you say the right words, poof!

What is the sacramental word, then? Perhaps it can best be explained
by referring to the greatest exponent of the idea in the early centuries of
the Christian community's life, St. Augustine. Augustine had two
obsessions which run right through his whole life's work. The first was
time. How do you make sense of yourself over time? You were you when
you were six years old. Now you are you at twenty or forty or sixty. In one
way, you are obviously not who you were at six, and yet, in another way,
you are the same self. How are you *you* over the course of a lifetime? With
such a concern constantly at work in his mind, it is not surprising that
Augustine wrote what is the first attempt in the western world at
autobiography, his *Confessions*. In light of the great conversion experience of his life, Augustine was confronted with the fact that what he
thought and how he lived at twenty and what he thought and how he

lived at forty were very different. Was he one person? Or was there a young Augustine and a middle-aged Augustine who really had very little in common? What made him a consistent self over a long period of time? That question fascinated him. I shall be back to it shortly.

The second of Augustine's obsessions was communication. He was a rhetorician by trade. For most people today rhetoric simply means inflated speech, but for the ancient world rhetoric was what we might call communications theory. It was the study of how one could communicate clearly and persuasively to others. In the immensely sophisticated, intellectually self-conscious, politically differentiated, economically complex ancient world which was also pre-printing press, rhetoric was immensely important. Communication of ideas and information was by the spoken word. So in the ancient world, rhetoric was the *sine qua non* for taking part in public life. If you were not a good speaker, you could not participate in the interchange of ideas in the public forum, because you could not put an article in a newspaper or circulate a paper. The only way to communicate ideas to a large number of persons was through public speaking. And if you could not do that persuasively, you were simply out of the game.

His background as a rhetorician laid the foundation for Augustine's lifelong concern with the question of how an idea, an image, an emotion in me can be communicated to you. How can you hear what I mean? And how can I know that what I meant is what you heard? The question is relatively easy if I am talking to you about some third object, say a pen, because we can both see it and point to it. When I say, "The pen is black," you can look at it and reply, "Yes, it certainly looks black to me." But how can I explain to you exactly how and why I feel happy? Or the precise kind and degree of sadness I feel? Or exactly what I mean when I say that I love you? Or what I experience when I say that I am worried or frightened? In these cases, there is nothing outside to which we can both refer. There is only an experience *internal to one of us*. We have all had the experience of describing to someone an important personal experience only to realize at the end of the conversation that the other person has not really understood what we were talking about at all.

Augustine was convinced that the attempt to express ourselves is central to every human being, that it is the constant activity in which every human being is engaged throughout one's whole life. The attempt to speak himself or herself, to say, "This is who I am, this is what I think and what I feel, what I like and what I fear," is the central work and motivating force of every human life. Everyone is constantly engaged in an attempt to say who she or he is.

This is the attempt to speak one's word, one's *verbum*. Augustine held that the great word which everyone tries to say or act out, the great *verbum* which everyone attempts to communicate, is "*me*." And we are all trying to express ourselves all the time. Our *verbum* may be spoken in non-verbal language, of course, what today we might call "body language." People express themselves in great decisions, such as whom they marry, how they raise their children, what professions they enter, and in small choices, such as what they wear, how they sit, what games they play, what tunes they whistle. And, of course, they do it every time they open their mouths or pick up their pens.

But although we are all engaged in the attempt to speak our *verbum* all the time, Augustine was convinced that we never do it fully and finally. There is never a time when you and I finish saying who we are, and that for an obvious reason. Here we intersect with what I described as Augustine's first obsession. You can never finish saying who you are because you never totally *are*. You are never completely *there*. You are always strung out over time. There is no single moment when everything you have been, everything you are, and everything you will be are all present. What you were, totally and completely, at sixteen is no longer here, because you are no longer sixteen.

The only person who could fully and finally, perfectly and completely, say who he or she is would be someone who *is*—fully and finally, perfectly and completely. To say who you are completely, you would have to know who you are completely. And to know who you are completely, you would have to be who you are completely. You would have to be completely there, not spread over "have been" and "will be," but simply there in the present moment. In other words, to say who you are completely, you would have to be out of time, i.e. you would have to be eternal. And now you see where we and Augustine are going. The only one who can say the *verbum* which is completely, finally, absolutely and always adequate, only God can express God's self perfectly.

And so Augustine points to the beginning of the gospel of John (which, of course, he is reading in Latin) where it reads, "In the beginning was the Word (*Verbum*), and the Word was with God, and the Word was God" (Jn. 1:1). "Precisely," said Augustine. From all eternity God has been endlessly saying who God is. God endlessly speaks God's Word, God's *Verbum*, but in God's case, God's *Verbum* is absolutely and perfectly who God is. So God's Word is God.

We noted that Augustine spoke of the Trinity as the lover, the beloved and the love between them. Another set of terms could be the speaker, the speech, and the delight in the speech. From all eternity, God has been saying who God is, and God is simply tickled with who God is. From all eternity, God is the speaker of the Word, the Word which is spoken, and the acceptance of the Word, God's self-recognition, the divine "Yes, that's me!" When speaking of the Trinity as lover, beloved and love, we said that the universe is what happens when God chooses to love outside the Godhead, i.e. that we exist because God loves us. In terms of the Trinity as speaker, word and delight in the Word, we may now say that the universe is what happens when God chooses to speak outside the Godhead, i.e. we exist so that God can converse with us.

II. GRACE

God's communication of God's self, God's Word, addressed to us in our world is what we mean by grace. "Grace" is simply theological shorthand for the self-communication of God outside the Trinity. God is an eternal explosion of love. From all eternity, God is the giver of the gift, the recipient of the gift and the gift itself. If God chooses to give God's self outside the Trinity, the universe is what happens.

God's love is absolute. You cannot get more or less of it. When God gives God's self, God gives God's self completely. You can choose to accept it or reject it. You can choose to open yourself more deeply to it or close yourself to it. You may be able to celebrate it more fully at one time in your life than at another. But God's love is given to you totally, absolutely, perfectly at every moment of your existence. If it was not, you would not be. The only reason anything exists at all is because God loves it.

Notice, I am using the word "anything," not "anyone." God loves this book as much as he loves you or me; otherwise it would not exist. The difference between the book and me is that I can recognize and accept that I am loved and the book cannot. It is not the case that we humans are loved and the rest of the universe is not. Remember: God is the absolute mystery which grounds and surrounds all that exists, so everything is loved absolutely or it would not be. Grace is the perfect self-gift of God, the divine *agape* outside the Trinity. Thus everything that exists rests on grace. Everything is engraced, although not everything can accept grace and not everyone who can accept grace does.

In his later writings Rahner spoke about "the grace at the roots of the world." The universe is rooted in grace; it rests on grace; it would not exist except for grace. So grace is everywhere. This claim has very important consequences. Often we speak of the sacred as though it were a quite separate realm from the secular. What I am suggesting is that there is no secular realm, if by "secular" we mean "ungraced" or "unrelated to the *agape* of God." There may be many aspects of life about which we do not customarily use religious or theological language to talk about our experience, but that does not mean that those realms of experiences are ungraced. Every aspect of our being is ultimately connected to the fundamental question of where we stand in face of the *agape* of God.

Perhaps we should attend to a second meaning of the word "catholic" which is not often enough noticed. The root meaning of "catholic" is "universal," as we know. But by calling our faith "universal," we do not simply mean that it is supposed to embrace the whole world. We also mean that it embraces the whole person, that there is no aspect of your life or mine with which this faith is unconcerned. Were we to maintain that our faith is irrelevant to some part of our lives, private or social, then we would be saying that our faith is less than catholic. There is no aspect of life which is secular, in the sense that it is unrelated to what we believe about God. We can say this because we believe that there is no part of our lives, no aspect of our experience, no domain of society, nothing in the universe, which is unloved by God, ungraced. Anything ungraced is not secular, it simply *is not*. What is not graced does not exist. For to exist is to be loved by God.

III. THE INCARNATION

There is a problem, however, with the image of the universe as that which is created so that God can speak God's Word to it: we do not speak God's language. God, as it were, speaks God-talk, and we speak human-talk. God speaks God's Word to us, and we cannot grasp it. How is God's self-expression, God's *Verbum*, the eternal Word to be become understandable to those who are not God? The Word must be translated. How is the absolute Word of God translated into human speech? The prologue to John's gospel gives its famous answer: "The Word became flesh and lived among us, and we saw his glory" (Jn 1:14). Jesus of Nazareth is the human translation of the Word, God's perfect self-expression in human terms. Jesus is the Word said in our language, in a way we can grasp as human beings. To use a phrase from Rahner once again, we have been created to be "hearers of the Word."

If God eternally speaks God's Word and the Word is translated into Jesus, how is that Word addressed to those of us who do not happen to have been born in Palestine nineteen hundred and some-odd years ago? If, in order for the Word to be spoken to us in human terms, Jesus must live among us, deal with us as one human being deals with others, communicate with us as we communicate with one another, how is it possible for Jesus to be the Word of God fully expressed in human terms *now?*

The answer is, "In the same way that anyone communicates with others." What is the medium, the tool, if you like, that allows you to communicate with someone else? Your body. We communicate with one another through our bodies. My lungs propel air through vibrating vocal cords and lips and teeth; my face and hands gesture; my arm moves and my hand grips a pen, or my fingers peck away at a keyboard. No body, no communication. As human beings, we communicate with one another through our bodies, whether we use our bodies to sing or dance or paint or sculpt or play music or build buildings or speak and write to one another. And exactly what we no longer have access to is Jesus' physical presence. His body is not here. Or is it?

IV. THE BODY OF CHRIST: THE COMMUNITY

The body of Christ is present here and now. How often have you heard the church called the body of Christ? By the church, I mean the community of persons gathered together publicly by faith and even more by the attempt to live as *agapic* gift, following the example of Christ. That community is spread through time and space and is realized everywhere that people come together to commit themselves publicly to live in accord with the *agapic* message of Jesus.

God's perfect self-expression is his *Verbum*, translated into human terms as Jesus. Jesus' masterpiece, his self-expression, is the community. We have discussed in Chapter 2 that God exists as the foundation of our capacity to form relationships. God is least wrongly understood as ground of our interaction with one another. God's Word, God's self-communication, is experienced by us as a community, through our sharing of ourselves with one another.

But the church, too, is ceaselessly engaged in the attempt to express itself. What are the church's self-expressions, its *verba?* The church's primary self-expressions are the *agapic* lives of its members, the way we live with and for one another, the ways we accept grace into our lives and thank God for the divine self-gift. The doctrines of Christianity flow from that experience of Christian living and prayer; they are the community's attempts at understanding itself. As such, they are very important and necessary for living the community's life as fully, i.e. humanly, as possible. For as we said in the previous chapter, action and reflection on action can never be separated from each other. But one cannot reflect on an action without first acting. And one cannot understand the community's life without living that life. Think of your own experience. How did most of us first learn the faith? Not by reading the Bible or the catechism, I am sure, but through our parents, family, friends, the people among whom we grew up. We came to Christ first through other people, through the community in the widest and richest sense, and so through the church. Only then were we introduced to scripture and the doctrines of Christianity, which help us understand what this community of which we are members is about.

There are occasions in which the church communicates itself most effectively, when it says as deeply, intentionally and intently as it can, "This is who we are." Those occasions are called sacraments. The Roman Catholic community holds that there are seven such occasions when the church most fully expresses who and what it is. Now, I hope, it is obvious why Rahner maintained that "word" is the operative element in the sacraments. The Word of God in the flesh is Jesus of Nazareth; Jesus' great word is the church, and the church's great words of self-expression are the sacraments.

V. SYMBOL

If we follow the theme of self-expression from the Trinity to the incarnation to the church to the sacraments, we realize that sacraments are symbolic expressions of grace. "Symbolic" is, of course, a loaded term. I suspect that few words have had as much written about them in contemporary philosophy as "symbol." Symbols are the way we express our apprehension of mystery. When we are confronted with what is too vast, too glorious, too beautiful, too terrible, too joyful, too painful—quite simply, too real to be able to name exhaustively—we enter the realm of symbols.

Now, it is important to recognize that symbol is not sign. Sometimes we use the words "sign" and "symbol" as if they refer to the same thing, but it is necessary to notice the different ways the terms are used here. A sign is an arbitrary pointer to something else. For example, when you see a red light, you know that you should stop. But there is nothing intrinsic to a red light meaning stop. In another society or in a different context, a blue light could just as well mean stop. It is simply an arbitrary reminder.

A symbol, by contrast, is both more important and more basic. A symbol is an external expression rooted in what it points to. It does not point *out* to something else as a sign does. It points in to its own depth to express what cannot be expressed in any other way. For example, an embrace is not an arbitrary sign of affection. You could not decide that, to express the same thing, you will kick the person instead. Tears and laughter are not arbitrary signs; they are outward expressions rooted in the inward experiences they symbolize.

One of the classic descriptions of sacraments in theology, going back to our friend St. Augustine, and employed often by St. Thomas Aquinas, is that "a sacrament effects what it signifies." That is to say, a sacrament makes what it signifies real, makes it effective by manifesting or symbolizing it. This is how we understand the claim that sacraments cause grace. If we remember that grace is God's self-gift outside the Trinity, obviously it becomes blasphemous to claim that a sacrament somehow "makes" God give God's self. How then do sacraments "cause" grace? By signifying, both Augustine and Thomas would reply.

Perhaps an example will help. Imagine yourself in a dentist's waiting room. No one else is in the room at the moment. In the next room you can distinctly hear the high-pitched whine of the drill which sends shivers down your spine. You are thinking how much this visit may hurt and wondering how much it may cost. Now, in the background, Muzak is tootling along. But you are paying no attention to the Muzak whatsoever. Indeed, if after you left the office someone were to ask you if any music had been playing, you would be able to answer with perfect truthfulness, "I didn't hear a thing." After some time has gone by, another prospective dental patient comes into the waiting room and sits down. And after a few moments, the newcomer leans over to you and asks, "Excuse me, what is the name of the tune that's playing?" For the first time, the music goes on *for you*. The music was always there, but it needed to be pointed out before it was there for you. It was present but without effect. (I presuppose, please note, that there is something to be pointed at. If the other person in the waiting room asks you "What is the name of that tune?" and there is no music playing, I would advise that you get out of the waiting room as rapidly as possible!)

(The wise and attentive will have noticed that there my analogy of sacramental causality to the experience in the dentist's waiting office limps somewhat. The wise and attentive will recall that a symbol points into itself, whereas a sign points out from itself. So, if sacraments are symbols and not signs, my analogy is inaccurate. It would be better if we told the story in such a way that, instead of someone asking "What is that tune?" the dentist's receptionist in the next room accidentally brushes the volume-control on the Muzak so that suddenly the music roars at you. That would be the music calling attention to itself, which is how a symbol functions, rather than being pointed at by something else. My compliments to the wise and attentive reader.)

This is what is meant by the statement that a sacrament effects what it signifies. A sacrament makes grace effectively present for you by bringing it to your attention, by allowing you to see it, by manifesting it. Sacraments presuppose the omnipresence of grace, the fact that the self-gift of God is already there to be manifested. But because grace is always present, it frequently goes unnoticed. Any thing, any person, place, event, any sight, sound, smell, taste, or touch that causes you to recognize the presence of grace, to accept it and celebrate it, is a sacrament, effecting what it signifies.

So, then, how many sacraments are there? There are as many sacraments as there are effective pointers for you to the grace which lies at their root. Everything is potentially sacramental. Grace is always and everywhere present, for whatever is not engraced does not exist. But we are not always capable of seeing the grace and so accepting it. This is beautifully expressed by a line in Gerard Manley Hopkins's poem "Hurrahing in Harvest": "These things, these things were here and but the beholder/ Wanting." Grace is always present. What is needed is someone to notice it. Sacraments are those persons, places, things and events which cause you and me to notice the grace. A sacrament reveals to you that inner luminescence, like a dying coal lit up from the inside. It allows you to see into its depth, to see the grace in which its existence is rooted, to acknowledge and celebrate God's absolute love for all that exists.

If everything is potentially sacramental, then some persons, places, things and events may be sacraments for one person rather than another. Perhaps the most obvious example is that of marriage. When you marry, your spouse will, I hope, be a sacrament, maybe even the sacrament, to you. He or she will not be a sacrament, at least in the same way, to me. Your children will, I trust, be sacraments to you. To other people they may be noisy little horrors, but to you they will be manifestations of the ultimate goodness which undergirds the universe. We all have our own personal sacraments, many, many of them, if we are fortunate and attentive. But I suggest that there is one fundamental sacrament for each of us—the self.

I have mentioned earlier Jonathan Edwards' definition of true virtue (or true holiness, which is really closer to what Edwards was discussing than the usual meaning of "virtue" today) as the consent of being to being, which I suggested includes the consent of finite being to being finite, being limited. The recognition of our finiteness, of the full reality of our limitedness, can be terrifying. No one is able to guarantee that he or she will live out this day. We are unable to say with certitude that you or I will be alive at the close of this year. We are limited in our time, limited in our energy, limited in our abilities, limited in our intelligence.

And to say, "Yes, I choose to be this finite being, and it is good so to be," to consent to the goodness of radically limited being—that is the key to true holiness or true virtue, in Edwards' language.

Now, if this is true, and I think it is about the truest thing I know, then I suggest to you that the primary sacrament, the sacrament closest to you, is you. The being whose finitude you must affirm as good, as rooted in the perfect *agapic* love of God, is you. The primary sacrament for you is your *self*, as the primary sacrament for me is my *self*. The beginning of true holiness, the discovery of the sacramentality of the universe, is to be able to look in the mirror and say, "I know how radically limited that creature is, and it is good." This is no small thing; it may be the work of a lifetime—to affirm the goodness of your existence, not as an ideal, but as you concretely are. It is the revelation of the fundamental sacrament. Once you see yourself as sacramental, as rooted in grace, as good, then the sacramentality of everything else lights up. And until one can see one's self as sacramental, I do not think that one can ever appreciate the sacramentality of everyone and everything else.

VI. ENCOUNTERING THE OTHER

What is the response when you start to see the world, including first and foremost yourself, as sacramental—when you become, to use Hopkins' term, a beholder? The response is love. Even before faith, love is the effect of sacramental vision. Faith comes later, for faith always carries an element of knowledge within it, and knowledge depends on love. We do not know and then love what we know. We love and then are able to know. Love is always primary. Of course, the love which is the effect of sacramental vision is *agape*.

This is the point at which I should try to explain further what *agapic* love means. To do so, I must invoke what will at first seem a dry-as-dust phrase from St. Thomas Aquinas. But as you unpack the phrase it becomes richer and richer. Aquinas gives a wonderfully insightful definition of *agape* or, as he translates it into Latin, *caritas*: it is, he writes, "the effective willing of the good of the other."

The most striking point to notice about this definition is how counter-cultural for us it is. For most late twentieth-century North Americans, love is an emotion. But Thomas does not make any reference to emotion in his definition. Not that he thought that emotions, or passions as he called them, are bad. But all those tender, warm, affectionate feelings which we usually describe as love, however wonderful and good they are, are not the meaning of "love." For they come and go. Emotions do dissipate. No one can feel warm and affectionate all the time. But this does not mean that love dissipates—unless we mistakenly identify love with a particular kind of emotion.

Thomas' definition describes love as an act of the will. Love is a choice we make. That is very different from the way we think and talk about love most of the time in our culture. We talk about someone "falling in love," about love "hitting you" like Cupid's arrow, as if love were something that happens to you, an experience in which you are essentially passive. Thomas' definition says quite the opposite. Love is an activity into which you enter willingly. Emotion—fascination, attraction, desire—may hit you, and sometimes being hit by it may feel perfectly wonderful. But such emotions are, at most, the accompaniments of love. At core, love is to will the good of another in such a way that you effect, i.e. make real and active, that good for the other. To paraphrase St. Thomas, *agapic* love is willing the good of the other person and acting to make that good real for him or her.

Unless we understand love in some such way, much of the gospel sounds like absolute nonsense. For example, how else can one possibly understand Jesus' command, "Love your enemies; do good to those who hate you" (Lk 6:27; Mt 5:43–44 NJB)? If one thinks of love as tender and affectionate emotions, then the command is simply crazy; one will not regard one's enemies with tender, warm affection, no matter how much one twists one's emotions or lies to oneself. Indeed, if one takes "love" to mean "be affectionate toward," then the command may be immoral, for if the enemy is unjust, one ought not be affectionate toward one who acts unjustly. But if one understands that affection is an occasional accompaniment of certain forms of love and that the core of love is always the active willing of the good of the other person, then it may be difficult to love one's enemy but it is not nonsense. Then the command of Jesus is that one actively will the good of all persons, not just one's neighbors but also one's enemies. Your enemy, who may be unjust and undeserving of affection, may hate you for attempting to bring about his or her good, but you must still act in that way. It is not a question of how you feel but of what you choose and how you act.

As a celibate observer of marriage in our society, I think that the notion that love is essentially a matter of emotion, that it is something which happens to you rather than a choice that you make and an act that you choose, has terribly destructive consequences in marriage. If you think of love as something that you "fell into," then you can—and almost certainly will—"fall out" of it. If love is something that happens to you, then you cannot guarantee that it will continue to happen. No one could ever make a marriage vow, were love something that happens to one rather than something one chooses to do. If love is a passive experience, you do not have the ability to tell another person that you will love him or her till death do you part. There is no way that you can promise that, if love is an emotion. For if love is an emotion that came without your expecting it, it can leave without your expecting it. You can only make a vow to love another always if love is something that you can choose to do.

Thomas' definition of love as an act of the will which chooses to effect the good of the other requires two qualities (at least). The first is wisdom. You can never know with certitude what the true concrete good for the other is. You must always try to perceive what that concrete good may be so that one can act to bring it about, recognizing that you may be wrong. You must be ever ready to revise your idea of what the other's good is.

The second quality which love demands is courage. Courage is required because, when you discern as wisely and carefully as you can what you believe to be the other's good, it may not be what the other wants at the moment. For example, a little child wanders toward a hot stove with outstretched hand, and its parent says "Don't touch that!" and pulls its hand away. From the child's point of view, mommy or daddy is a monster who will not let the child do what he or she wants. From the parent's point of view, pulling the child's hand away from the stove was an act of love. The parent discerned what was best for the child and acted to achieve it, although the person for love of whom the parent acted does not appreciate or accept it. Loving *agapically* is a very tough business. Were the love of which we are speaking *eros*, I would want to make you feel good because it will make me feel good, and so I will do whatever you want done and tell you whatever you want to hear. But this is *agape*, so I will do what I think you truly need done and tell you what I think is the truth. And if you do not like it and do not want to hear it, I love you so much that I am willing to let you be furious with me.

Both wisdom and courage are required because love recognizes the other as genuinely *other*. The great Jewish philosopher earlier in the twentieth century, Martin Buber, suggested in his most famous work, *I and Thou*, that human experience is composed of two fundamental relationships. He described them as "I-thou" and "I-it" relationships. An "I-it" relationship is one in which the other exists for my gratification, my pleasure, my ambition, my power. Whenever the other becomes an extension of me or a means to my ends, however good those ends may be, then I have turned the other into an It.

I suspect that many of us really think of life as a motion picture in which we star. I am the lead in "Life: The Movie" and all of you are bit parts. Some people have fairly large supporting roles, but I am the star. In our imagination, when we walk into a room the background score (probably by John Williams) swells. (I must confess, whenever I see people walking on the street or the campus wearing headphones, I think "Ah, the twentieth century! Now we can live our lives with a soundtrack.") Far too often other people are reduced to *my* parents, *my* brother, *my* sister, *my* spouse, *my* child, *my* friends, *my* employer, *my* employee, *my* roommate, *my* teacher, *my* student—they are all *mine*. They exist insofar as they are in relationship to *me*. They play roles in *my* life. Anyone and anything can become an it for me, a tool for my use.

By contrast, it is grammatically impossible to make "you" the substantive with the possessive "my." You can be my friend, my student, my associate, my colleague, but I cannot make you "my you." You are incapable of being owned, of being reduced to an aspect of my life. You are always sovereignly mystery to me, not something that I can manipulate or control or absorb into my framework. You remain you, always the other. So an "I-thou" or "I-you" relationship is one in which I recognize the other as a true other. Buber offered the superb description of God as "the You which by definition can never become It." I like that description very much. In the deepest sense, God can never be *my* God. God is always God. God can never be cast in the role of the cavalry which comes to my rescue when I am in trouble, the one who shows up when I need help, the comforter when I am worried. God may, in fact, act in such a way, but God can never be reduced to the correspondent to my need. God is God, the absolutely other.

As everyone and everything can become an it, everyone and everything may be a you. As we have said before, anything that exists does so because God wills it into being, loves it into being. Everything that exists has its own integrity as that which God loves. Thus everything that exists is always a you, the other which exists not because I can make use of it but because God has looked at it and seen that it is good. What do you do when you encounter the fundamentally other, i.e. when you see someone or something not as an extension of you but like a fading coal, lit up from within? There is only one thing you can do: love it. You see it as God sees it—in itself, as it is, good—and so you do what God does: you love it.

The Christian theological tradition speaks about "the beatific vision" and the joy of that vision. I suggest that we not think of the beatific vision as our seeing God "face to face," as if God were another one "out there" at whom I look. Rather, think of the beatific vision as a way of seeing. That is to say, instead of our seeing God, we begin to see as God sees. And what God sees is a universe in which everything is you and nothing is it, everything is that other which God is loving into being as good. Seeing the world that way is union with God. God is not the object of beatific vision, God is the style of vision which is beatific. We are called to see as God sees. Sacramental vision, being a "beholder," is a step toward beatific vision. It is seeing everything as revelatory of the grace which lies at the root of the world.

To love another person agapically is to see that person as God sees him or her. You see as God sees and do what God does. You are acting as what you are, the image and likeness of God who is love. As I have mentioned before, God is not some great big person "out there" loving and being loved; God is what you experience when you love as self-gift; God is the ground of your capacity to love that way. God is the reason you can love anyone else. God is the reason anyone else can love you. God is, as it were, the glue that holds the universe together. That glue is absolute delight in its existence, perfect joy in its being. God has looked at creation and seen that it is good. And we are invited to look at the universe in the same way and make the same judgment. Whatever the occasion—the person, thing, place or event—which enables you to see the other as other and so to see the other as held in being by absolute love, that occasion is what we mean by sacrament. This idea of sacramental vision is what holds together the whole Catholic understanding of Christianity. It is what is catholic about being Catholic.

The great communal sacrament in the Catholic Christian tradition is the eucharist. In it we discover who we are and where we are going. We can not understand agapic life apart from the eucharist which is its great embodiment, and so in the next chapter we say something about the way in which the tradition has envisioned the eucharist.

Word, Sacrament and Community
RESPONSE BY RONALD WHITE

In the community I grew up in, there was a saying which went something like, "Jive talks, action walks." It is very expressive of the general lack of faith I and many in my community had in words. I'm sure this is understandable given my background as an African American raised in the south of the 1950s. Going to my segregated school I heard regularly about the Constitution and equality and the inalienable rights of all. But to me it was just so much jive talk. My everyday experiences totally contradicted these noble sentiments, these fine words, of our founding fathers.

The one exception to my skepticism was church. Here James'

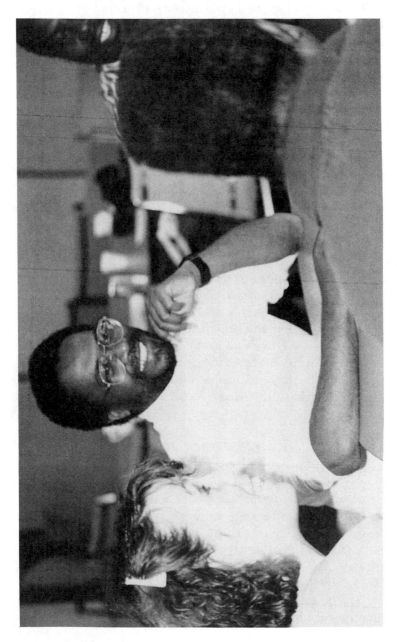

Ron White in a discussion with others involved in the Campaign for Human Development

admonition to "Welcome the word that has been planted in you and is able to save your souls" was taken seriously and acted on. So growing up, church was the one place where I consistently saw word and power come together. Action and faith united. Whenever it was evident that this happened I felt blessed and whole and filled with hope. And it wasn't just me. The whole community raised its voice with renewed vigor and commitment. Believe me, we needed it to deal with the daily insults of life, without turning to uncontrollable rage or despair, both of which are death. In contrast, the word of God we heard in church was literally life. I guess this is my experience of what Michael means by "sacrament." It was this word proclaimed and lived, which opened us as a community to the holy, to the unity of life, to God's infinite love. Of course, none of this was articulated in my early years. I just knew the words of the gospel were sustaining to me, healing, comforting to the community, and challenging to the status quo. This was after all the 1950s, a time of great change for my generation in the south.

Many years later while working for the Campaign for Human Development, I saw this word do the same for another very different community. Hearing their story was sacrament to me (i.e. it made real what it signified) and so I share it with you.

In 1992 I visited a community in East Los Angeles which had the highest density of low income housing in the city. There, amidst the problems all too typical of our urban poor communities—drugs, crime, gangs, drive-by killings—I encountered the clearest witness to the power of the gospel I had ever been privileged to see.

A small prayer group of Latinas ranging in age from 20 to 50 told me the story of how they won back their community from gangs and drug dealing with nothing more than faith in the gospel.

It seems that one night at their regular prayer group, they encountered the passages in Matthew where Jesus calms the storm (Mt 8:22ff) and calls Peter to walk on the water (Mt 14:22ff). As they reflected on these passages they began to speak of the storm in their communities. The storm's rage made this a community where no one dared sleep near a window at night, and in fact many had their children sleep under their beds for fear of stray bullets from the nightly gun battles. The storm's rage turned their street corners into open air drug markets where Mercedes and even limos paraded through hourly to purchase and corrupt. The storm raged such that these good church women who had started soup kitchens, housed homeless refugees from El Salvador, established a day care center and visited the ailing of the community, would not venture out at night, nor would their husbands. They were afraid of the youth on the streets day or night and often felt their community was not their own.

Make no mistake. I recognized this as a "profane" state of affairs. I knew it was not possible to find God's love or grace as long as this reign of terror persisted. This was their storm, and as they described it, it echoed its fear in my own heart as I listened. I know this kind of fear. It keeps the mind and heart in a very tight circle of concern, much like a dog chasing its tail. You follow what's immediately in front and life becomes dangerously simple; you do what it takes to stay alive. Though more chaotic and violent on a daily basis, it was not very different from my adolescent life in its consequences.

The more these good people prayed and talked, the more they began to reflect on Peter. Flawed as he was, he stepped out of the boat into the raging winds. Among the women I met that day, each denies being the first to say it, but each says someone said, "We have to leave the safety of the boat, if we are to be true to Jesus' call. If we act on Jesus' word maybe the storm will cease to rage." And they did. That very week they contrived to meet with the leaders of the gangs which terrorized their neighborhood. What they discovered over time was that these were their children. They were not the enemy, they were prodigal sons. They lived like "gangbangers" but they were the sons of their friends and even their own sons and daughters. From that point the relationship changed to one of "I-thou" between the women and the gangs.

They also saw the outside drug buyers as the major source of their children going astray, getting into fights, being lured away from decent work, and killing each other. They told me how they would sit on the street corners day and night reading scripture to each other and breaking into song whenever cars came up to buy drugs, calling out the license plate numbers and surrounding the cars at times. The cars stopped coming. The open air drug markets closed in their neighborhoods. The gangs, though angry, didn't quite know what to do with these women who talked to them as if they truly loved them. The women got the priest to sponsor a gun turn-in program, and find good jobs for those who gave up dealing drugs and went to school. They founded a co-op, "Homeboy Tortillas," and employed their own youth. Many good things came out of their willingness to, as Maya Angelou would say, "Step out on the word of God" and leave the boat. Essentially they moved their community from profanity to grace.

In James' letter we read, "Be doers of the word and not just hearers only" (Jas 1:21–22). These women reaffirmed for me the power of God's word. Once again what before could only be vaguely hoped for, or cynically dismissed as utopian, became real because of allowing the word to take root and life. This is sacrament, this is life in God's community of faith.

Questions

1. Define "sign" and "symbol" and describe the differences between them. Give examples to illustrate your definitions.

2. What are St. Augustine's two obsessions? How are they interrelated?

3. Explain what is meant by the "self-expression" of each of the following: a) God, b) Jesus, c) the community. Explain how the latter is somehow dependent on the former.

4. How many sacraments are there? Explain your response. What does it mean to say that the self is a sacrament?

5. How does Thomas Aquinas define the sacraments?

6. What are the two qualities which love demands? When the believer possesses these qualities, how are relationships then transformed from an "I-it" relationship to an "I-thou" relationship?

7. What does it mean to "see as God sees" or "to love as God loves" or to enjoy the beatific vision? Give examples.

Journal Questions

8. Return to your journal entry on Zossima's advice. Recollect all the people whom you encountered in that exercise of faith. Knowing what you know now, would you say that you "love" those whom you came into contact with? Write for five minutes without lifting your pen on the people with whom you work or worship, asking yourself, "Do I love you?" Take a break and then write for another five minutes on what it means to love as God loves or to see all people as God sees life.

9. How do you experience "all life as sacramental"? Come up with as many stories or examples of sacramental moments in your life as you can, using Ron White's reflections as an example.

8
EUCHARIST: COVENANT, THANKSGIVING AND DESTINY

> We eat the body of Christ to become the body of Christ.
>
> *—St. Augustine*

If someone who knew nothing about Christianity were to attend a celebration of the eucharist, what would he or she think it was about? I suspect that, if we asked such a person afterward what he or she had seen, the person would reply, "Well, you Christians certainly do make a great deal of fuss about eating some bread and drinking some wine together." And he or she would be right: the eucharist is, first and foremost, the act of eating and drinking together.

That is very important, because in the great reverence which we believers have for the eucharist, we can lose sight of the central symbol. And if we do, we misunderstand the great enactment of the most important claims of Christian faith. For it is striking, is it not, that while we affirm that the risen Lord is present in our midst, the manifestation of that presence which we call the "real presence" is through something which is eaten so that we are nourished, something which is drunk so that we are refreshed.

The heart of what we believe about the eucharist is the Christian claim that the fullness of the presence of God is found in Jesus of Nazareth, God's perfect self-expression in human terms. In this human life and death and destiny is found the Word of God, so if one wants to know what Christians mean by "God," one should look at that life, death and destiny. One must, therefore, look to the presence of Jesus today, and one of the symbols of his presence, the one which we call his "real presence," is the eucharist. So, the eucharist shows us who Jesus is and Jesus shows us who God is. If the eucharist is something that is given to me for my nourishment and refreshment, then Jesus' real presence among us is as the one who is eaten up by others. The human self-expression of God is the one who gives himself so that others may have life, because the absolute mystery which we call God is least wrongly understood as pure and perfect self-gift.

118

This means that real participation in the eucharist requires that we become self-gift also. Thus the eucharist becomes not only an expression of the communion of believers with God through Christ but an expression of our communion with one another and our dedication to others within and without the Christian community. And as a sacrament which "effects what it signifies," the eucharist does not only symbolize this communion and dedication, it makes it real.

I. COVENANTS

To understand the eucharist as the sacrament of Christian communion, we must see it within the pattern of covenants which form a trajectory to the last supper. In Genesis 8:15–9:17, after the great flood has ended and the waters have subsided and the ark with Noah and his wife and their three sons and their wives comes to rest on dry land, God calls them to leave the ship and resume life on the earth. And God proposes to enter into a covenant with these eight people who are, in the story, the only ones left alive in the whole world. So Noah builds an altar and chooses certain animals and birds which had been with him and his family in the ark as burnt offerings and sacrifices. Burnt offerings or holocausts are offerings in which the gifts were given entirely to God; this total giving was shown by the complete destruction of whatever was offered so that no one else could ever use it, thus making it God's alone.

The other form of sacrifice mentioned here is a communion sacrifice, an offering of which part of the gift was destroyed as God's share and part was cooked and eaten by those making the sacrifice. A communion sacrifice was a symbolic meal shared by God and the human beings offering the sacrifice. Even today sharing a meal with one another is a sign of hospitality, friendship and trust, and it was a very important expression of solidarity in the ancient near eastern world in which those who first told this story lived. For eating with someone meant that you were being taken into that person's family, being brought under his or her protection. So to have a meal with God meant that you were now under God's protection. You were God's people, and those who attacked you had to answer to God.

God blesses Noah and his family and commissions them to repopulate the earth. All the goods of the earth are given to them for their sustenance—with one significant exception: they may eat nothing with blood in it. Why? Well, remember that the tellers of this tale were people with rather primitive notions of biology. Using common sense, they had noticed that when an animal had all its blood within its body, it was likely to be alive and kicking, but if all its blood drained out, it was dead. They therefore drew the perfectly natural conclusion that blood equaled life. But life belongs to God. If only God could give life, then life was God's property, as it were. Blood, i.e. life, does not belong to human beings, it belongs to God. The theme of blood in connection with the formation of covenants remains very important throughout the trajectory from Noah to the last supper.

God initiates a covenant by announcing, "I am now establishing my covenant with you" (Gen 9:9 NJB). The parties to this first covenant are God and Noah and his descendants, who in the context of the story are all of humanity. The terms of the covenant are set forth: God will never again destroy the whole world. And God establishes a sign as a permanent reminder of this covenant—the rainbow. "When the (rain)bow is in the clouds, I shall see it and call to mind the eternal covenant between God and every living creature on earth" (Gen 9:16 NJB).

The second of the great covenant-formation stories is that of the covenant with Abraham. Abraham and Sarah abandon their home in the Chaldean city of Ur, giving up their gods and their families, to follow God, who will bring them to a new land where they are destined to become the founders of a great people. Their descendants will become a great nation and will inherit all of the new land. And all goes well, save for one thing: the clock is ticking and they have no children. How are they to become the ancestors of a great nation when they have not even one descendant and, in the story, Abraham is approaching ninety and Sarah is not getting any younger either? Once again, God assures Abraham, "Do not be afraid, I am your shield and I will give you a very great reward." "Lord God," Abraham replied, "what use are your gifts and promises as I am going my way childless? You give me no offspring" (Gen 15:1–3). God promises the old man that his descendants will be as numerous as the stars of the sky. And, although Abraham trusts God's word, he asks how he can *know* that he will father a people who will possess the land which has been promised. And so God offers him a covenant.

The way of forming this covenant is rather bizarre. At God's direction, Abraham assembles a number of animals and birds, halves them, and arranges the halved carcasses in two lines, each half opposite the other. Then God solemnly repeats his promise and, in the form of a blazing fire, passes between the pieces of the animals. This strange ritual was apparently a fairly common way of formally sealing treaties and compacts of great importance in the ancient near east. I suppose we might think of it as a highly ritualized way of doing what children today do when they promise something with the words, "Cross my heart and hope to die!" Effectively that was what participants in these rituals were saying: "If I do not remain faithful to this covenant, may I end up like these animals!" The participants were pledging their lives as guarantees of their fidelity. So the Hebrew story uses this ancient near eastern treaty-formula to describe God's sealing the covenant with Abraham.

The sign of this covenant is circumcision (Gen 17:4–14). Notice how the permanent reminder of the obligations of the covenant has changed from the story of Noah. Then it was a phenomenon out there in the heavens, the rainbow. Now it is an actual physical operation on the person's body. The sign is still physical and external, but personal.

Notice, too, how the role of the participants in the covenant has changed. In the story of the covenant with Noah, the human participants say never a word. In this story, by contrast, Abraham is the one who actually provokes the covenant. It is asking how he can *know*, how he can be certain of God's promise, that leads to God's granting of the covenant. The terms of the covenant also become more explicit than in the earlier pact with Noah. First, God promises that he will fulfill his words to Abraham: his descendants will inherit the land. On the other hand, Abraham and his descendants will remain faithful to their covenant with God as *their* God. And although there is no direct reference to blood, clearly a lot is spilled in the halving of the sacrificed animals' carcasses. It is in their blood that the covenant is sealed.

But the most important and famous of the covenants in the Hebrew scriptures and the one which sets the pattern for Israel's relationship with God throughout the rest of its history is that formed through Moses in Exodus 24. After God has rescued the tribes of Israel from slavery in Egypt, Moses leads the people to Sinai. There he ascends the mountain and spends forty days and forty nights alone with God. When he descends, he brings with him the law which God has given him for the people, the summary of which is the ten commandments. Then he gathers the people together and proclaims to them all God's ordinances. And the people respond, "We will perform all the words that God has spoken" (Ex 24:3). Moses directs the construction of an altar at the foot of the mountain made of twelve stones, one for each of the twelve tribes. Then he orders that burnt offerings and communion sacrifices be made. Moses takes half the blood from the sacrificed animals in basins. The remaining half he pours over the altar. Then, after once again reading the laws, the so-called book of the covenant, to the listening people who affirm their promise of obedience, Moses takes the blood collected in the basins and sprinkles it over the assembled people. As he does so, he tells them, "This is the blood of the covenant which God has made with you" (Ex 24:8). And then, in a wonderfully mythological conclusion to the great scene, Moses and the elders of Israel go up the mountain and eat and drink with God. Down at the base of the mountain everyone else symbolically shares a meal with God through the communion sacrifices.

In this story of covenant-formation, the human participants play a major role. Moses proclaims the law, Moses commits it to writing, Moses directs the arrangements for the sacrifices. And twice the people are called upon to voice their approval and acceptance of the terms of the covenant. The human participation in this covenant is certainly much greater than the one with Noah. The terms of the covenant have now become very explicit, indeed. The terms of this covenant are fidelity to the whole of the Mosaic law. And the sign of this covenant is to be the people's obedience to that law. The covenant signs have moved from some physical phenomenon out there, the rainbow, to a physical operation performed on one's body, circumcision, to the way one lives one's life. And the whole is celebrated with a shared meal with God and with one another.

The "blood theme" is very prominent in this covenant-signing. Part is poured over the altar, and part is sprinkled on the people once they promise obedience. Recall that blood equals life. Part of the life is God's, so symbolically it is poured over God's throne, the altar. And part is the people's, so it is sprinkled over them. God and the twelve tribes have become blood relatives. They share the same life. In a sense, it is like children swearing blood-brotherhood. It is the symbolic statement that Israel is related to God by blood.

The Mosaic covenant in Exodus 24 is the great touchstone of God's relationship with Israel. Again and again, throughout the Hebrew scriptures, we hear the reminder that Israel must be faithful to that covenant. If the people have disobeyed and broken the covenant, then it must be patched up again. But in the later prophets, after the time of Jeremiah (late seventh and early sixth centuries BC), the way the covenant is cited changes. The covenant is like a sheet or a patchwork quilt which has been torn and patched and torn and patched so many times that nothing is left of the original to patch. But because of God's mercy and fidelity, one hope remains: that God will send a new Moses who at some point in the future will establish a new covenant between God and the people. And so expectation turns toward the one who is anointed by God for this task, the Anointed, the Messiah in Hebrew, the Christ in Greek. The later prophets turn our attention to a new covenant which will not be inscribed on stone tablets like the Mosaic one, but on our hearts, a covenant that can never be broken.

The Messiah will do what Moses did: he will mediate a covenant. And not surprisingly, eager expectation of the Messiah and the new covenant became especially linked with the great annual celebration of deliverance and covenant, the Passover, the yearly repetition of communion sacrifice when God's people share a meal together. The Messiah will give us the new covenant at Passover. And after six hundred years from the time of Jeremiah, six hundred years of waiting and hoping, a group of people—fishermen from Galilee, a reformed tax collector and collaborator with the Roman government of occupation, an ex-member of a revolutionary party, and women who have accompanied them, come to celebrate Passover in Jerusalem with an itinerant rabbi who has said and done such remarkable things that they have begun to wonder whether he could be the Messiah. And when they gather on the night of the Passover meal, the rabbi about whom they have such hopes starts the dinner by saying to them, "I have been eager to eat this Passover with you" (Lk 22:14). Obviously, anyone raised within the Jewish tradition in that situation had to think, "This is it! Tonight's the night! He will seal the new covenant with us tonight." And that is just what he does.

When those first disciples of Jesus said that Jesus was the Messiah, they meant that he was the mediator of the new covenant. And when they tried to understand what he had done with them at the Passover meal the night before he died, they thought in terms of a covenant-sealing in the tradition of Noah and Abraham and most especially Moses. Were we able to ask those earliest Christian brothers and sisters of ours what we are doing when we celebrate the eucharist, they would undoubtedly reply that we are sealing the covenant. That is certainly the language and imagery the New Testament uses to describe Jesus' actions at table with his friends the night before his execution.

II. THE EUCHARIST AS THE SEALING
OF THE NEW COVENANT

There are four accounts of the institution of the eucharist at the last supper—in the gospels of Matthew (Mt 26:26–29), Mark (Mk 14:22–25), and Luke (Lk 22:15–20), and the earliest account of all, that in Paul's first letter to the Corinthians (1 Cor 11:23–25). Paul's account, Matthew's and Mark's are basically very similar. Luke's has a number of significant differences. But for our purposes all are agreed that Jesus followed the customary ritual of the Passover meal but modified it by changing the words spoken at key moments, thus changing the significance of the celebration.

The first of those changes is in the prayer of blessing recited by the host at the Passover supper over the unleavened bread. This is a kind of solemn "grace before meals" when the host would take a loaf of unleavened bread, break off a piece, and pass the loaf to the first guest, who would in turn break off a piece and pass the loaf to the next person at the table. The blessing which the host prayed recalled the bitterness of slavery in Egypt and their deliverance by God. In sharing the bread, those at table not only remembered their ancestors of long ago and all of those centuries of people whose lives connected them with the generation of the exodus, they united themselves with them and so with all generations to come who would eat that bread on that night until the Messiah should come. Thus it was an affirmation of union with one another, with those who had gone before them and those who would come after. The community gathered together for the Passover acknowledged and celebrated their communion with the whole covenant community past, present and future. It was probably at this point that Jesus changed the words of the blessing before breaking the bread and passing it around for each one to eat. Jesus said, "This is my body." In effect, he was saying that this bread is not only a reminder of the bread that our ancestors ate, this bread is me.

After the main course, a similar prayer of blessing was recited over the solemn cup of wine. Until that point in the meal, everyone would have had his or her own wine cup. But then a special larger cup would be placed before the host who recited over it a kind of "grace after meals." The blessing explained that this wine was a reminder of all the blessings God gave to sustain their ancestors and continued to give them. And by sharing this cup with one another, the guests participate in advance in the banquet of God's kingdom with the Messiah. Again, the people at table affirm their communion with all those who are members of the covenant over the ages. Then the host would drink from the cup and pass it around the table so that all the guests might drink from it. Almost certainly it was at this point that Jesus again significantly altered the ritual. He announced that this wine was his blood, the blood of the new covenant.

Jesus takes the rituals of the Mosaic covenant and gives them new meaning even as he celebrates them. The bread is still blessed as is the cup. But now eating this bread is not just union with our past and future, it is union in and with him. Drinking this wine is no longer a reminder of the covenant established at Sinai and an expression of hope in a covenant which will someday be given, it is the blood that seals the new and everlasting covenant now. In changing the meaning of the Passover supper, he completed the trajectory which began with Noah.

Recall Moses' use of the blood of the sacrificial victims, half of which was poured on the altar, the sign of the presence of God, and half sprinkled over the people. Jesus echoes Moses' words, "This is the blood of the covenant" (Ex 24:8), when in presenting the cup to his friends at table he says, "This is my blood of the covenant" (Mt 26:28; Mk 14:24). The image of the shared blood, which is life, meant that God and the people shared the same life, they were blood relatives. But Jesus identifies the blood of the covenant as *his* blood. And he does not sprinkle it externally on us but gives it to us to drink, to take within us. His blood, his life, is in us. Thus, what was shown externally by Moses' action, that God and we are blood relatives, is internalized: Jesus' life now flows in our veins. What he said was, in effect, "What you are about to drink is my blood. Since blood is life, this is my life. I give it to you to consume so that you will live my life."

And what are the terms of this new covenant? Here John's gospel is important. The fourth gospel does not mention the institution of the eucharist at the last supper, although it is by far the longest account (all of chapters 13, 14, 15, 16 and 17 of John's gospel). But John's account is a detailed statement of the terms of the covenant sealed by the eucharist. The sign of the covenants between God and humanity moved from the rainbow to circumcision to obedience to the Mosaic law, from an external natural event to an operation performed on one's own body to the way one lived one's life. In John's gospel, Jesus gives as sign of the new covenant what one might anticipate from this trajectory. What is the sign that you belong to the new covenant? "This is how everyone will know that you are my disciples: that you love one another" (Jn 13:35). The sign of the covenant has moved from the rainbow outside us to the physical operation of circumcision to changed behavior and lifestyle and now becomes a wholly new motive. The motive for everything we do is to be *agape. That* is how everybody will know that we are members of this covenant. The external sign of the new covenant is the love of the community for one another.

And so John's gospel begins its account of the Last Supper with a gesture by which Jesus demonstrates *agapic* service. In some ways, I suspect, the Johannine counterpart to the eucharist in Matthew, Mark and Luke is the story of Jesus' washing the feet of his disciples. In the ancient near east, the first thing to do to welcome guests wearing open sandals and entering from hot, dusty, unpaved roads was to supply them water to wash their feet, almost like our offer to take their coats. If yours was a wealthy household, you might have a servant wash their feet for them. But when the guests arrive in the upper room for the Passover supper, Jesus does not merely provide water and towels for them, he greets them by washing their feet. He will be their servant. This is the seal of the covenant, that we serve one another as he has served us.

Thus, were we to ask that first generation of Christians what they were doing when they came together to eat and drink the eucharist, they would have answered that they were sealing their covenant with God and one another. They were sealing the covenant together. And that is what we do. However much, however often we have failed to live the life of self-gift which is the central core of Christianity, we can seal the covenant once again. That is why we begin our celebration with a confession of sin. It is because we have sinned that once again we need to recommit ourselves through the communion sacrifice of the Lord to the common life and agapic love we share with God and one another.

How seriously our earliest brothers and sisters in the faith took this community-forming function of the eucharist is shown by Paul's very strong statements about it to the Christians in Corinth. Paul tells them that he can offer them no congratulations on their communal meetings which, from what he has heard, do more harm than good (1 Cor 11:17). For when they gather to celebrate the lord's supper they do so in the course of what we might describe as a pot-luck supper, i.e. people bring dishes for a common meal. But the Corinthian Christians are not sharing what they bring. Each little circle of friends eats what its members have prepared, and there are grave inequalities. The wealthy members eat very well and the poor members have little or nothing to eat. "Have you such disregard for God's community that you can embarrass those who have less than you?" Paul questions (1 Cor 11:22). He then recounts what he has been told about the institution of the eucharist at the meal the night before Jesus died and concludes, "Anyone who eats the bread or drinks the cup of the Lord unworthily is guilty of the body and blood of the Lord. All are to examine themselves and only eat of the bread or drink from the cup after doing so, because a person who eats and drinks without paying reverence to the body is eating and drinking his or her own condemnation" (1 Cor 11:27–29).

When Paul warns those who are not reverencing the body of Christ, he does not just mean that they do not believe that the eucharistic bread is the body of Christ; he means that they are disgracing the community which is the body of Christ. If people at the eucharist are creating factions and embarrassing the poor, then when they claim to eat the supper of the Lord, they are actually killing Christ: they are guilty of the body and blood of the Lord. To make the sealing of the covenant and celebration of communion with God and one another into an occasion for envy and fighting and separation is to kill Christ as surely as to have driven in a nail on Calvary. That is Paul's very strong judgment: split the community and you murder the Lord.

Our communion with the Lord and our communion with one another mutually condition each other, i.e. we are united with one another because we are united in Christ, but we are also united in Christ because we are united with one another. It is a theological "chicken-or-the-egg." Neither is primary; each is the cause of the other. This might seem strange, indeed, unless we remember that according to the deepest insight of the Christian tradition, God is least wrongly thought of as the relationship of pure and perfect self-gift and that Jesus is God expressed in human terms. So we cannot come into relationship with God save by being related to others. For God is not a baptized version of Zeus, some great big person "out there" to whom we are related. God is found in our relatedness to others. And at the same time, we cannot truly give ourselves in the service of others without being in communion with God—even if we do not acknowledge the fact—because God is the ground of our capacity to love others. As we said earlier, the two great commandments are two sides of a single coin: the love of God *is* the love of neighbor, and vice-versa.

And so the eucharist is our communion with Christ because it brings us into communion with one another, and vice versa. Or to put it another way, the eucharist makes the church. It seals our covenant, our compact with God precisely by uniting us into one community. This is why just before we actually eat and drink the Lord's supper, we exchange a sign of peace with one another. This is not just an additional ritual in the celebration; it is our enactment of an essential condition for participation in the eucharistic meal. We cannot receive the body of Christ without being in communion with our brothers and sisters. The sign of peace is our expression of union with one another so that we can come to the table of the Lord. For "if you are bringing a sacrifice to the altar and there remember that your brother has something against you, leave your sacrifice at the altar, go and first be reconciled with your brother, and then come and offer your sacrifice" (Mt 5:23). Only when reconciled with our brothers and sisters can we take part in the communion sacrifice at the altar, for we cannot be part of the Lord unless we are part of one another.

The eucharist is the sacrament of this twofold communion, and as a sacrament it makes effectively real what it symbolizes. This is what St. Augustine meant when he explained why we Christians celebrate the Lord's supper: "We eat the body of Christ to become the body of Christ." That is, we eat the eucharist in order to become a community, the church. The eucharist is not about personal devotion if by that we mean my one-to-one private relationship with God. It cannot be because whatever the experience of God may be in the Christian tradition, it is never private. The experience of God is always communal because "God" is the name of a relationship. And so the eucharist is always an experience of community.

III. GIVING THANKS AND
CELEBRATING OUR DESTINY

Why call the central and primary Christian communal celebration the eucharist? The word "eucharist" comes from the Greek verb *eucharistein*, meaning "to say thank you." But why call it that? Why not call it "the offering" or "the communion sacrifice" or "the meal"? Why "the thanksgiving"? It is certainly true that the synoptic gospels and the first letter to the Corinthians use that verb when they describe Jesus "giving thanks" as he blesses the bread and the cup of wine at the last supper (Mt 26:27; Mk 14:23; Lk 22:17 and 19; 1 Cor 11:24). But I suggest that there is a very profound reason why "thanksgiving" has become the term by which we most often refer to the central act of Christian worship: it is the best description of our position before God.

If the absolute mystery which we call "God" is least wrongly thought of as perfect self-gift, then we stand before that mystery forever as the recipients of gift. Not only is everything we have ultimately God's gift to us, not only is the fact that we exist a gift, but we exist precisely in order to be able to be given the gift of God. We can give nothing to God which God needs. Indeed, as many of the thanksgiving prayers of the liturgy remind us, whatever we can give to God has first been God's gift to us. We are not created to be gifts to God; we are created to be recipients of God's gift to us. That is why we are. And the primary gift which God gives to us is God. So our basic stance before God is gratitude. We are the part of creation which is given knowledge and tongue to say what all creation longs to say: thank you.

How are we to give thanks? By being what we are—the image and likeness of God, and therefore those who exist by giving themselves away. The great Christian act of worship names the fundamental Christian way of living. We live by loving our brothers and sisters, and the name for living in such a way is "gratitude," "thanksgiving," eucharist. And so again we encounter the fact that celebrating eucharist is the reflex of our relationship to one another.

But the eucharist not only tells us who we are, it tells us where we are going. we proclaim that in the eucharistic celebration the bread and wine become the real presence of Christ. Is there any intrinsic difference between the little bit of bread and few drops of wine which we use to celebrate the eucharist and the bread which you popped in the toaster this morning or the wine you will have with friends at dinner this evening? If the bread and wine we use at the eucharist can become the fullness of the presence of Christ, why not that slice of toast or that glass with friends? All bread is incipiently the presence of Christ; all wine is potentially the reality of the risen Lord. And if the bread is the product of seed and soil and rain and sunlight, if the wine is the result of vine and soil and sun, then are they too not capable of being transformed into the eucharist? If one little bit of the universe, the bread and wine we employ in the celebration, can be the fullness of Christ's presence, then all the rest of the universe can be. The eucharist is the tip of the iceberg. It is the first step in the transubstantiation of all creation.

In the prayers for the feast of Corpus Christi, the annual feast of the eucharist, there is an antiphon whose Latin text has often been set to music, *O sacrum convivium*, "O sacred banquet." In it the church describes Mthe eucharist as the *pignus futurae gloriae*. A pignus in Latin is a pledge, a down-payment, a first installment. So the eucharist is hailed by the community as the first installment of future glory. It is the first stage in the process which St. Paul describes in what may well be the most breathtaking passage in the New Testament: at the end, having made all things subject to himself, Christ will overcome the last of his enemies, death, and then he will turn the whole kingdom over to his Father, "and God will be everything in everything" (1 Cor 15:24–28). The eucharist is the destiny of the universe.

In the forty-five minutes or an hour in which we celebrate the eucharist, we enact the meaning of existence. For the Christian claim is that the key to existence is self-gift: if you give yourself away, you exist truly, and if you do not give yourself away, you edge closer and closer to non-being. We enact our fundamental stance before God. For we are always the recipients of the gifts of God, and, most of all, of the self-gift of God. And we enact our destiny. The universe is to become the fullness of God's presence in Christ, and the eucharist is the first installment of that transformation. We are the part of creation which is privileged to know, to accept and to celebrate that destiny, that self-gift which is God. According to St. Paul (Rom 8:19 and 22), the whole creation is groaning to say what must be said but cannot be said until we human beings say it: Thank you.

I have spoken about sacramental vision and, in this chapter, eucharistic vision. I have used the word "vision" to suggest that sacramentality is a way of seeing the world, and certainly celebrating the eucharist is a new way of beholding who we are and what our destiny is. Seeing ourselves and the world differently is, of course, a consequence of revelation, of the fact that something new has been shown to us. And theology is a way of trying to reflect upon that new say of seeing. Having vision—or, as I shall suggest in the next chapter, expanding one's imagination—is both the pre-condition and the result of living agapically. That is what we must close by considering.

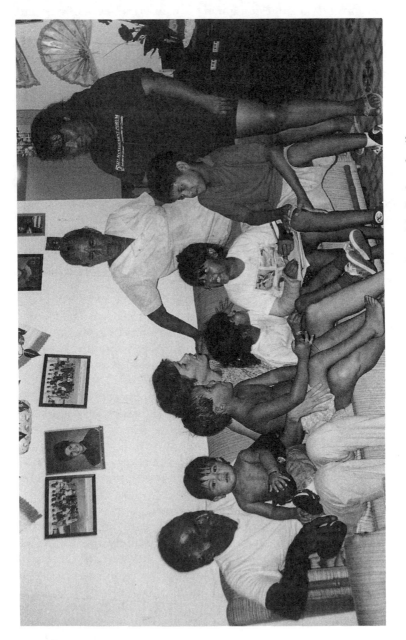

Maria Teresa Gaston-Witchger with some members of the Pacheco family

Eucharist as Being Fed by the Poor
RESPONSE BY MARIA TERESA GASTON-WITCHGER

As a young adult and later as a newlywed, I worked in the archdiocese of Milwaukee in parishes developing ministry among Hispanics. My favorite times were when I was just somebody who was hungry—just a person who needed a meal, or a person who needed to be welcomed. Then I could receive. I loved being in that stance of receiving the self gift of others—with humble people sharing their food, in their homes and part of their lives—because I could reflect back to them the gift of who they are: people of faith, love, beauty, wisdom and such generosity.

Since we moved into a farmworker ministry in southwest Florida, it has been a great joy to make it possible for university students as part of their education to be able to meet and form relationships with farm workers, working side by side in the fields and staying overnight in their homes. My husband, John, and I host students for an alternative spring break week where they worship with the local community in Creole or Spanish, work in the fields, volunteer at various schools or agencies, learn about farm worker life and agriculture, sleep on the floor at the parish catechetical center and for two nights live with Hispanic and Haitian families in their homes.

Their encounters with the people of Immokalee, Mexicans, Haitians, Guatemalan Mayan, farm workers, restaurant owners, homeless men, hospice patients, eager children and, most of all, the families who host them for two nights, moved them to gratitude and awe. In addition, the week of living together is a profound experience of community. The students come together out of a common desire to give of themselves and grow through interaction with people very different from themselves. They form great friendships. This year, the Notre Dame group was very diverse culturally within themselves including Chinese, Afro-Cuban, Mexican-American, Colombian, and a child of deaf parents. They learned and received so much from each other each day. It's wonderful to witness and be part of God's presence in these encounters.

One encounter between a host family and a Notre Dame student particularly highlights Himes' eucharist as gratitude and *agape* theme. This year I prepared a group of children for first communion through the parish catechetical program. Weekly, for thirty weeks, I picked up two children, Mario and Karina, living down at the other end of our street, to attend the sessions. Mario was in fourth grade and his sister, Karina, though nine, was only in first grade, having recently arrived from Mexico with her grandmother who had been raising her.

I occasionally was early to pick them up, and went into their home and chatted with the grandmother, Nicolasa. I came to know the extended family. Eight adults and nine children lived in a simple, rented three bedroom house paying $250 a week. Nicolasa took care of her grandchildren while her adult children worked in the fields and the older grandchildren attended school. The adult children, in various states of transition or crisis, had no residency documents, yet wanted to better themselves even though they were hampered by high rent and irregular work.

After six months of the school year, I felt welcomed in this home, and it occurred to me that they would be a great family to host a student on the alternative spring break experience. I wondered if they would do it. When I found out several of the Notre Dame students spoke Spanish, one night I stopped by the home and asked the family if they would be hosts for a student for two nights. They looked at each other and the oldest son said, "Yes, we'll take one." The children were excited. The grandmother said we might not have much to eat. "Does it have to be special?" she asked. "Whatever you ordinarily are cooking," I said. "The students want to experience you as you are in your daily living, not in books."

Several weeks later the students arrived and were gathered to preview the week and select their host family. I described the various host families to the students, and right away Erika expressed a desire to stay with Karina at the Pacheco home.

When the night came for the students to move to their families' homes, I asked Erika if she would mind being last so I could stay and eat with her and the Pacheco family. I wanted to make sure Erika would be all right and make sure the family felt accepted even if Erika didn't like the food. (She professed to be a vegetarian and was not used to hot food.) When we arrived we were warmly greeted by all three generations. The children, ranging in age from three months to eleven years, circled us eagerly. They cautiously touched Erika's long, blonde hair and quickly began to pellet her with questions about where she lived, how long she could stay, and more. Erika expertly juggled giving them the attention they craved, while at the same time getting to know the adults in the family.

Nicolasa invited us to come sit at the table to eat. The table was small and had three chairs around it, none of which matched. I noticed several small cockroaches scaling the wall behind the stove. I wondered and worried how Erika would handle the situation. A big pot spewed steam on the stove, and Mario and Karina's mother, Alma, stood near it heating tortillas while her sister, mother of the infant, quietly poured drinks.

Watching Erika allayed my fears. I marveled at her ability to relax and engage Alma and Nicolasa in conversation and then to genuinely enjoy the bowl of stuffed banana peppers on broth which we were graciously served. She didn't seem nervous at all. I marveled too at the ability of this struggling undocumented family to so generously welcome a stranger to their table. When we finished our food, which was delicious, we gave up our seats so others could sit around the table and have a chance to eat.

I don't remember if we prayed or not, but I do remember how holy it was, bringing different worlds into communion with one another. All meals like the eucharist have the potential to do this, Himes reminds us, but how rare it is we share meals with people very different from ourselves. There is so much that keeps the poor at a distance from most of us. Himes writes that "if we are not part of one another, we cannot be part of the Lord." When we do take risks, share stories, build a friendship, we become part of one another, and we become part of the Lord. This is the *agape* experience that so touches the lives of the students who visit Immokalee and the families who host them.

I am so grateful to have been a part of this sharing around Alma and Nicolasa's table. They serve as Jesus served. They put themselves into the food they prepare and make possible a taste of the covenant with God and with all creation in the sharing of a meal. Himes describes eucharist as the "tip of the iceberg," and I wish he would say that the iceberg is around women's tables. It is such a natural extension to have women serving as hosts and presiders at the table of the Lord just as they do at their own tables.

The next day, Erika went to work in the fields with five of the adults in the family. She worked by their side, picking tomatoes for seven and a half hours. When she joined her fellow students on Thursday, her body ached from her labor yet her face was radiant. The worn Polaroid pictures the family gave her symbolized how deeply Erika had won their affection.

Two weeks later, I asked the Pacheco family if they would be willing to host one more student. This was the first year we ran two separate "Taste of Mission" groups and I just had to ask them to do it again. This time a young Mexican seminarian stayed with them. He had been studying in Pittsburgh and feeling very cut off from his culture. He had not wanted to come on the trip, but was asked to by his spiritual director. After staying with the Pacheco family he told me he felt alive again. It was Holy Week. During a party after the Holy Thursday trilingual eucharist, Nicolasa came in to say that Alma would like to invite the whole group over for an Easter meal Saturday night. I was astounded. This the poorest of all the host families wanted to go all out for this group of mostly northern gringos. What could be more sacramental? God was so present and alive in that exchange, reaching out, the offer of tamales for twenty-six foreigners at a table that seats three. That must be what happened with the people in the gospel story of the multiplication of the loaves and fishes. Jesus helped people to trust that what they had was good enough to share and then there was abundance.

Himes states that eucharist not only tells us who we are, it tells us where we are going, as did the covenants of old. The week of spring break is for me a taste of the "reign of God" Jesus ushered forth and calls us to—where injustice will end, and we will all see each other as the beloved of God that we are.

When students arrive in the homes of their host families in Immokalee, they come hungry and tired after sleeping in cars and on the hard floor of the catechetical center at church. They are the ones with language and cultural limitations and feel their powerlessness. In need, they call forth the generosity, warmth, and love of the families they stay with. When the students eat and stay to sleep in the home, they honor the family by accepting their gifts. The students find themselves overwhelmed by how much they feel accepted and loved. The mutual acceptance is a gift from God, reveals God present, and the response is overflowing gratitude. In my ten years living and serving in Immokalee, I don't think anything else I have done has been more worthwhile.

Questions

1. Name and describe each of the covenant treaties from Noah to the last supper. Note the differences between them. (You may want to develop a chart to do this exercise.)

2. What is the significance of the alterations Jesus made in the ritual of the Passover meal at the last supper? How and why are these significant?

3. How do we participate in the life of Christ in taking of the bread and wine at eucharist? How is it that we "become what we receive"?

4. Why is the eucharist, or thanksgiving, not called "the meal," or "the sacrifice"? Why does Himes define eucharist as "the destiny of the Universe"? Choose one person with whom to share this insight. What is his or her response?

Journal Questions

5. What does the eucharist in all its parts mean to you? When has it been most meaningful? Least meaningful? How do Maria Teresa's insights guide your connections between the eucharist and your daily life?

6. Read Hebrews 11:7–12:4. What meaning does this now hold for you. Write your response.

7. Write a covenant of your own with God intended to embrace not solely the commitments of your own life, but your family, your worshiping community, and some global commitments. How would you like this covenant to read? How is the covenant a mutual agreement between you and God?

9
DOING THE TRUTH IN LOVE

Without a vision, the people perish.

—Proverbs 29:18

I. IMAGINATION

"We too often and too quickly think of a will that submits and not enough of an imagination that opens itself," wrote the philosopher Paul Ricoeur some years ago. His point is very well taken. Too often and too easily we tend to emphasize the need for conversion of the will when what is really required is an expansion of the imagination. We speak too readily, and assume that those who disagree with us are selfish, and so we set out to convert their wills, to exhort or preach or shame or badger them into selflessness. But the cause of their opposition or lack of interest may more often be their inability even to imagine how the world looks and what it feels like to someone else. They cannot imagine other ways of living or acting or dealing with people. They assume that there are certain ways of responding in a situation: they can do A or B or C. And so they decide on C because it is better than the alternatives. The problem is not a selfish or wicked will; they are doing the best that can be done, in their view. The problem is that they often have too narrow a view. They are limited to A or B or C. They cannot begin to imagine D through Z. They are not closed or uncaring. They simply lack imagination.

The word "imagination" may give some pause here. Unfortunately, we have reduced the meaning of that word to playing with impossibilities. The great poet (and no mean philosopher) Samuel Taylor Coleridge sought to distinguish "imagination" from what he called "fancy" and we might call "fantasy." "Fantasy" (or "fancy") is the combination of things or places or feelings which we do not usually associate, e.g. flying carpets, talking animals, castles in the air, etc. But "imagination" is a creative faculty, according to Coleridge; it is, in his term, "vital" or life-giving. It is the capacity to embody the abstract in the concrete, literally, "to make an image" of what has previously existed only as a concept. To cite another great poet, it is what Shakespeare describes so wonderfully in *A Midsummer Night's Dream*: "The poet's eye, in a fine frenzy rolling,/Doth glance from heaven to earth, from earth to heaven,/And as imagination bodies forth/The form of things unknown, the poet's pen/Turns them to shapes, and gives to airy nothing/A local habitation and a name" (V, 1, ll.12–17). Imagination "bodies forth" what has previously been unknown because unrealized and unacted; now it is given "a local habitation and name." Unlike fantasy, imagination is not about escaping from reality; it is precisely about making things real.

When a possibility is perceived as "not being real," we cannot be outraged or even surprised that people do not choose it. To return once more to St. Augustine, there is a passage in his *Confessions* (8, 11) which I think has been insufficiently noticed. When Augustine describes with painful intensity his struggle to choose the life which he had become convinced was the right one, he discovered that he was unable to will the change. He knew what he ought to do and, on some level, he wanted to do it. But, as he puts it, his will was divided. He willed to live differently, but he could not will to will it. When he strove to break with his past life, the memories of his old loves, his former mistresses, appeared before him, asking whether he could really bear to live without them. In his highly dramatic presentation, he speaks of a kind of vision in which he saw chastity personified who encouraged him to move to a new way of life by showing to him examples of men and women of various ages and stations who had successfully incorporated their sexuality and lived chaste lives. Only then was he able to advance to a point where he could effectively will his choice.

What Augustine recognized as he looked back on his conversion experience was that no one can choose nothing over something. His past life was real; he had experienced it and could imagine it. By contrast, the new life which he wanted to choose was a blank; he had not experienced it, had no picture of it before him, and so could not be moved to it. What was needed was to body forth the form of this thing unknown, to give it a local habitation and a name, to make it vital, to realize it, literally, to make it real—in short, to imagine it. Only when he could imagine it, i.e. have an image of it before him, could he choose it because only then did it become a real possibility for him. There would have been no point in exhorting Augustine to change his way of living; he already knew that he should. Nor was there any point in trying to shame him into doing so; he was already crushed by shame. What was necessary was to enable him to imagine the alternative as real. Paul Ricoeur is correct: the prime issue was a matter not of will but of imagination.

There is a statement attributed to Stalin that the death of one person is a tragedy, but the death of a million persons is a statistic. What Stalin cynically recognized was the importance of imagination. The death of one person whom I can see, whose name I know, whose grieving family and friends are there for me to meet, has an impact upon me because it is an experience which I can imagine; it is concrete and real. And so I may feel some responsibility or desire to act in the face of that person's death. But when you tell me that there are thousands who are dying of some disease or as the result of a natural disaster or a war, the number is too great to be imagined, to be made real to me, to be rendered concrete, to be bodied forth. And so I shake my head and sigh, "How sad, how terrible!" Tell me of thousands of homeless persons in the United States, and my reaction is, "What an awful thing!" Show me or tell me of one particular homeless person, and I may feel called upon to assist him or her. This is why we respond to pictures on television of people dying of famine. It is not that we were unaware of the situation before; it was that the dying had no faces. Now they are not the abstract "people"; they are "those people," and so we mobilize to assist them. Television has helped us to imagine them. Stalin was right, you see. Increase the numbers of the dead and we cannot imagine them. And so they cease to be a tragedy and become a statistic.

There are as many reasons not to serve others, not to act for justice, not to assist those who suffer, not to defend the oppressed, as there are reasons to do so. We may not act because of insecurity about our own value and ability, and so we worry that we cannot do anything effectively. We may not act because of a placidity which is thinly separated from sloth or because of a selfishness that is damnably close to malice. But sometimes—I am inclined to think many times—we do not act because we cannot imagine what to do.

What emerges from Paul Ricoeur's statement is that the key issue may be to induce people to imagine new possibilities of life, of interaction, of community, new possibilities which they have never seen before, of ways in which human beings might live with other human beings, the ways in which a society may be fostered, the ways in which God and we interact. But there is an important caution: the call to expand the imagination is not an invitation to romanticism. I remind you of the difference between imagination and fantasy: the first deals with reality; the second does not.

II. SEEING WHAT IS THERE

Within the Christian tradition there is an ascetical tradition. Now, usually the word "asceticism" summons up images of fasting and silence, sacrifice and mortification. But the asceticism which is necessary for every believer, and crucial for all who seek to engage in any form of service, underlies all the forms which it has sometimes assumed, many of which now look simply bizarre to us. Indeed, sometimes what we usually think of as asceticism can be merely a distraction from the true ascetical calling.

Friedrich von Hügel, one of the wisest and most perceptive Catholics of his time, in an address at Oxford in the first years of this century, asked his hearers who they thought was the greatest example of asceticism in the nineteenth century which had just ended. Von Hügel answered his own question in a way which must have shocked his religious audience: he suggested that his choice was Charles Darwin. He explained that Darwin's infinite patience in years and years of painstaking study of the development of the beaks of various species of birds or the interbreeding of certain varieties of orchids or the shape of barnacles required a self-denial, a setting aside of the self which could be described in no way other than asceticism. For Darwin had been engaged in an attempt to see what the truth of the development of species was. He was trying to see what was there.

And that is the point of asceticism. Asceticism, self-denial, is not a form of masochism; that is a psychological aberration and requires a psychiatrist, not a spiritual director. Nor is it a way to please God, who is not a sadist enjoying the pain of creatures. Asceticism is not designed to punish oneself or to master oneself or to inure oneself to pain. Asceticism is the necessary discipline for knowing the truth. The point of self-denial is to get oneself sufficiently out of the way so that one can see what is the case. Ascetical discipline enables us to see things as they are, not as we would like them to be or as we hope them to be or as we fear them to be, not in a way that makes us feel better or that meets our needs or accords with our expectations. To get out of one's own line of vision so that one can see what is there—that is the purpose of asceticism. And I suggest to you that asceticism is necessary because, if we believe that God is the truth, then we must be devoted to seeing the truth.

In the fourth gospel Jesus describes himself as the truth (Jn 14:6) and tells Pilate that anyone who hears the truth hears his voice (Jn 18:37). If the perfect self-expression of God in human terms is the truth, then truth can never lead us away from God. Rather, the truth is where we experience the presence and action of God. The quest for what is real and true is movement toward God. Therefore, if Christians are called upon to be anything, they are called to be realists. We are not interested in what makes us feel good, we are interested is what is the case. We are interested in the truth.

This is, of course, the point of distinction between hope, which is a virtue like joy, and optimism, which is a morally neutral state like happiness. Optimism, like happiness, is a pleasant state, nice if you have it, but if it evaporates, it is of no ethical significance. Christianity does not—or should not—make us happy and optimistic; it does claim that among the signs of the Spirit in our lives is that we are joyful and hopeful. Hope does not put a rosy glow on reality; hope deals with reality even when it has no particular glow whatever. Hope deals with what is there in the belief that God is at work even when what is there does not make us feel good or raise our spirits. Christianity should produce clear-eyed realists, not cock-eyed optimists. True faith has nothing to do with jollying people along. It has everything to do with facing the fact that things may be an utter and total mess, may be on the verge of going to hell in a hand-basket, with the conviction that God is at work in the mess.

Jesus was obviously filled with hope but had little use for optimism. He knew with great, indeed, terrible clarity what lay before him in his ministry—that he would go up to Jerusalem where he would suffer and die. And when Peter offered him facile optimism—"God forbid, Lord! Such things will never happen to you"—he rejected it curtly: "Get behind me, Satan! You are an obstacle to me, for you are thinking in human terms and not like God" (Mt 16:21–23; also Mk 8:31–33). Optimism soothes, "Everything will turn out fine, you'll see." Hope recognizes, "You will be nailed to a cross but in some way, God will triumph even in that." Optimism is on this side of the cross, hope is on the other side. One must confront reality.

Our decisions and choices are to be taken in light of the truth, the real, the case, not what we wish for or what would make us or others feel good. The way to reach the real is the consistent training of one's attentiveness to the facts. And that is asceticism—putting oneself aside so that one does not see everything else through one's own hopes, desires, wants or needs. Seeing things as they are, attending to what is the case— that is the goal of asceticism.

One of my favorite twentieth-century poets, W. H. Auden, has a splendid poem, sometimes entitled from its first line, "As I Walked Out One Evening." He writes of going for an evening stroll along the Thames embankment and overhearing two lovers below a bridge. The lover promises his beloved what, I suppose, every lover has promised since Adam and Eve, that "Love has no ending," although Auden further exaggerates the hyperbole: "I'll love you, dear, I'll love you/Till China and Africa meet,/And the river jumps over the mountain/And the salmon sing in the street./I'll love you till the ocean/Is folded and hung up to dry/And the seven stars go squawking/Like geese about the sky." But Auden hears what the lovers cannot hear, the inexorable voice of time: "But all the clocks in the city/Began to whirr and chime:/'O let not Time deceive you,/You cannot conquer Time.'"

Time will gradually alter everything; even the lovers' present infatuation will yield to the daily tasks and problems. "In headaches and in worry/Vaguely life leaks away,/And Time will have his fancy/To-morrow or to-day." In some of the most telling lines I know in modern English poetry, Auden describes the deep sense of the fragility of all things: "The glacier knocks in the cupboard,/The desert sighs in the bed,/And the crack in the tea-cup opens/A lane to the land of the dead." But this thoroughly unoptimistic poem is not without hope. It is a hope achieved through an ascetic confrontation with reality. "O look, look in the mirror,/O look in your distress;/Life remains a blessing/Although you cannot bless./O stand, stand at the window/As the tears scald and start;/You shall love your crooked neighbor/With your crooked heart."

I think that Auden provides one of the most beautifully apt images for true asceticism: to turn from the mirror in order to look out the window. We must train ourselves to stop looking at what are mere reflections of ourselves in order to see the world as it is. And when we do, the world as it is—a muddle of grandeur and tawdriness, love and selfishness, courage and cowardice, plenty and poverty, pleasure and suffering—is to be loved, not because we overlook what Auden calls its crookedness but precisely in its—and our—crookedness. To love the neighbor whom we see only through rose-tinted spectacles, an innocent, well-meaning and always grateful neighbor, is a pleasant diversion; to love the crooked neighbor with our crooked hearts, that is an experience of the *agape* of God.

III. DOING THE TRUTH IN LOVE

Living the Christian life of self-gift entails imagining the world in a new way. I do not say fantasizing about the world, for to live a self-giving life—which is, after all, the only way that life can truly be lived, if the gospels are to be believed—presumes an ascetical training so that we see the world as it is. This is why *agape* requires wisdom and courage. Wisdom is needed in order to try to discern what the true good of the other is, and courage in order to act to bring about the good even when it is rejected by the other. But imagination means realization, concretization, bodying forth what is otherwise an abstract truth. In other words, it is not enough to know the truth, one must *do* the truth.

The gospel of John tells us that "everyone who does the truth lives in the light" (Jn 3:21). The truth must be enacted. Ascetic discipline is the preparation for seeing the truth, but once seen it must be imagined, i.e. given concrete shape, "a local habitation and a name," in Shakespeare's words. That is what living in service to and with others does: it imagines the world in a new way. It envisions the world as what God has told us it is in truth—good and deeply, perfectly, endlessly loved. In Coleridge's words, such imagination is "the repetition in the finite mind of the eternal act of creation in the infinite I AM"; in my far less elegant terms, we imagine—make concrete—the world as God sees it.

The statements attributed to Jesus in the gospels and especially the parables are provocations to expand the imagination. "You have thought of God as creator and judge," he seems to say. "Now try thinking of God as a wildly over-indulgent parent, or as a shepherd who would rather abandon a whole flock than lose one lamb, or a woman who will take a house apart to find a missing coin. You have thought of your neighbor as your fellow-believer; now try thinking of the neighbor as a Samaritan helping a Jew who has been mugged. You have thought of the kingdom of God as a glorious reign of peace and justice; now try thinking of the kingdom as a mustard seed or a treasure buried in a field or a pearl worth more than all others." And we are not just to think of God and our neighbor and the kingdom in new ways, we are to imagine them, i.e. realize them, in new ways. We are not simply to know the truth, we must do it.

This is, I suggest, the way in which we must hear those very strange statements of Jesus, the beatitudes. "Blessed are the poor, for the kingdom of God belongs to them. Blessed are the gentle, for they shall inherit the earth. Blessed are those who are in sorrow, for they shall find consolation. Blessed are those who hunger and thirst for justice, for they shall be filled. Blessed are the merciful, for they shall find mercy. Blessed are the single-hearted, for they shall see God. Blessed are the peacemakers, for they shall be known as the children of God. Blessed are those who are persecuted in the cause of justice, for the kingdom of heaven belongs to them" (Mt 5:3–10). What are we to make of the claims which Jesus seems to advance? What kind of statements are they? Surely they are not descriptions; has anyone noticed the gentle inheriting the earth or those who hunger for justice being filled recently? Are they simply promises? Keep your fingers crossed and some happy day all this will come true. Surely not. I suggest that they might best be heard as hypotheses to be demonstrated. Imagine the world this way, live accordingly, and see if they do not prove to be the case. The beatitudes are challenges to our imagination. They are to be concretized in our lives so that they are not ideal truths but realized truths. They are not to be accepted or believed; they are to be done.

Living in service to others will inevitably become a salve to our own egos or an implied statement of superiority or an appeasement of our consciences unless we are constantly expanding our imagination. Then self-gift becomes both the cause of the expansion and its fruit. Because of our experience of self-giving love we can see the world in a new way, and because we see the world in a new way we can give ourselves away. This is why reflecting theologically on our experiences of trying to love *agapically* is so important; it expands (I hope) our imaginations. And the only way in which others may be drawn to live *agapically* is if they see *agape* as a reality, not simply a lovely ideal. They will see it if we embody it. To make it a *real* possibility for others, we must live it.

If we imagine the world and the neighbor sacramentally, then we must reverence the world and the neighbor. If we imagine our lives eucharistically, then we must live as self-gift. To re-envision the universe sacramentally requires us to act differently within it and toward it, and to live *agapically* requires that we discern what the true good of the other is which we seek to bring about. And this new way of acting, this process of discernment, must be discovered in conversation with others. For our doing of the truth, our active reimagining of life, is never purely private. Our imaginations can never be expanded on our own. They need the provocation of others.

This is one of the reasons our coming together as the church is so necessary to our service of others. For we need a circle of conversation partners who will expand our imaginations. The wider, the richer, the more varied the members of our circle, the more expansive our imaginations will be. And if the circle of conversation partners embraces people who are not of our culture and country, we will find our imaginations greatly enriched. If those we engage in conversation are not of our age and our moment in time, the need to open our imaginations will be all the greater. So a community which is both catholic, i.e. unbounded in space, and apostolic, i.e. extended through time, can provide an extraordinarily rich context for conversation. And that is what the church at its best (and it is not always at its best) can be: a circle of companions in conversation who are trans-spatial and trans-temporal. We do not have to talk only to people who are also North Americans and late twentieth-century. We can talk to Jesus and Mary, Peter and Paul, the authors of the gospels and of the first letter of John, to Augustine and

Thomas Aquinas, to Teresa of Avila and Thomas More, to Dante and Dostoevsky, to Marianne Moore and Emily Dickinson and Ludwig Wittgenstein and T.S. Eliot and W. H. Auden. For if the communion of saints means anything, it means that death does not interrupt companionship or conversation. And there is a conversation circle to expand your imagination!

And we need to talk with one another—not only for support and encouragement as we seek to serve others (although that is certainly immensely important), but so that we can name our experience as well and fully as we can, so that we can draw the deeper and truer connections between what we experience and what others experience, so that we can know the truth which we are doing. Theology has something enormously important to contribute to this conversation among those who serve their brothers and sisters: the deep claim of the Christian tradition that when we love another as selflessly as we can, what we are doing is the least wrong way to name God.

Biographies
Michael Himes and Collaborators/
Respondents in 1995

MICHAEL J. HIMES was ordained to the priesthood for the Diocese of Brooklyn in 1972. He was awarded with distinction a Ph.D. in the History of Christianity from the University of Chicago. From 1977 until 1987, he served as Dean of the Seminary of the Immaculate Conception in Huntington, New York, and from 1987 until 1993 was Associate Professor and director of the collegiate program in Theology at the University of Notre Dame. Currently he is Associate Professor of Theology and undergraduate director at Boston College. His most recent books are *Fullness of Faith: The Public Significance of Theology*, which he co-authored with his brother and which was awarded the Catholic Press Association Book Award in 1994, and the English translation of J.S. Drey's 1819 *Introduction to the Study of Theology*. His articles have appeared in many books and numerous journals here and in England. He has lectured widely in this country, in Canada, and in Europe.

STACY HENNESSY lives in Austin, Texas, with her husband Kevin and son Charlie and is currently serving as the director of campus ministry and instructor of religion at St. Michael's Academy. After graduating from the University of Notre Dame in 1981 with a degree in political science and international studies and being an initiatior of the Center for Social Concerns, Stacy served with the Holy Cross Associates in Chile as a volunteer. Upon her return to the United States, she served as director of a group living situation for severe and profoundly disabled women in South Bend, Indiana, before attending Weston School of Theology where she received a Master's degree in theology. From 1989 to 1994, Stacy served as a campus minister at Iona College in New Rochelle, New York.

REGINA WEISSERT lives in South Bend, Indiana where she is a longtime member of the Christian Family Movement. A widow and mother of four, a grandmother to ten, and a social activist, "Reg," who has traveled in Central and Latin America, is a board member of Catholic Worker house in South Bend, active in peace movements, and has assisted as a part-time staff person of the Center for Social Concerns.

Reg has worked closely with Monsignor John Egan and Peggy Roach both at Notre Dame and in Chicago to continue creative responses of the church to urban ministry concerns.

ANDREA SMITH SHAPPELL was an undergraduate at Notre Dame from 1975–79 and became involved in the courses and programs of Don McNeill, C.S.C. which linked faith with service experience. Continuing the exploration of this link led her to coordinate the Family Ministry Program for Catholic Charities in Gary, Indiana and to a year of volunteer service with her husband, Brian, through the social apostolate in New Orleans. She returned to Notre Dame where she received a Master's degree in theology in 1985. Andrea works at the Center for Social Concerns, coordinating the summer service projects from 1981 to 1984, and teaching courses which integrate theology with service experience from 1981 to the present. She and Brian have three children, Elizabeth, Eric, and Nicholas.

LOUIS M. NANNI is the executive director of the Center for the Homeless in South Bend, Indiana. After graduating from Notre Dame in 1984 with a B.A. in liberal studies and political science, Lou served for two years as a lay missioner working in a Santiago, Chile shantytown with the Holy Cross Associate program. Returning to Notre Dame, Lou received his Master's degree in international peace studies and since then has involved himself in many aspects of community affairs and social concerns. As director of the World Mission office for the Catholic diocese of Orlando, Florida, he worked extensively in the Dominican Republic in the areas of pastoral support and economic development. In 1991 he joined the staff at the Center for the Homeless, and has since then served on numerous boards, including the Board of Trustees at the University of Notre Dame. In 1993, the Northern Indiana Chapter of the National Association of Social Workers honored him as citizen of the year, and in 1994 the Notre Dame Alumni Association awarded him the Dr. Thomas Dooley Award for humanitarian service. He lives in South Bend with his wife Carmen Lund.

MARIA TERESA GASTON-WITCHGER, the interim program coordinator for the Southwest Florida Farmworker Project, lives in Immokalee, Florida with her husband John and sons Philip, Martin, and Luke. Born in Havana, Cuba, Maria Teresa grew up in the greater Milwaukee area and became active in Hispanic ministry as a young adult during the national process of Hispanic Pastoral Encuentros. After graduation in 1979 with a B.A. in theology from Marquette University, she worked with

Hispanic Youth Ministry in Detroit and Milwaukee until 1984 when she and her husband moved to the farmworker community of Immokalee. There she works with youth and families, more recently concentrating efforts in parenting education and women's support. In 1988 she earned a Master's in religious studies–Hispanic ministry from Barry University in Miami Shores, and since then has taught (in Spanish) courses in pastoral planning, leadership and group dynamics in schools of ministry throughout the southeast region. Currently she is involved in her children's education and works part-time with a popular education and organizing effort among farmworkers sponsored by Guadalupe Social Services where John is director.

DONALD P. MCNEILL, C.S.C., is a concurrent associate professor of theology, specializing in pastoral theology, and has taught in the theology department at Notre Dame since 1971. A graduate of Notre Dame in 1958, he received an S.T.L. from the Georgian University in Rome and a Ph.D. in pastoral theology from Princeton Theological Seminary. With Henri Nouwen and Douglas Morrison, he co-authored *Compassion: A Reflection on the Christian Life.* Don helped institute the Center for Experiential Learning (1977). Currently he serves as director of the Center for Social Concerns which he and others instituted in 1982. Don has collaborated with the Advisory Council of the Association of Catholic Colleges and Universities since 1977 in the development of models and programs of service and experiential learning and justice education which continue to increase. As a Holy Cross priest, he has collaborated on the enhancement of post-graduate volunteer service, especially with church-related groups in the USA and in Latin America. He, the Center staff, and Notre Dame continue to be engaged in a variety of ways in programs of international and national and community service/learning linked with the curriculum.

JAN PILARSKI has been involved in Catholic social action since her days as a student at Notre Dame. Volunteer experiences and courses offered through the Center for Social Concerns spurred her to become involved in post-graduate service in 1980 with the Holy Cross Associates in Oregon. Jan's volunteer work and subsequent experience as a community organizer led to her work with the social justice office of the Washington, D.C. diocese, where she organized and trained parishioners to act and reflect upon the gospel's call to service. During this time Jan also served as the diocesan director for the Campaign for Human Development, the U.S. bishops' anti-poverty program. Since moving to South Bend five years ago, she has co-taught courses in theology and social ministry through the Center for Social Concerns and at St. Mary's College, and serves as vice-chair of the Campaign for Human Development Advisory Committee. Jan and her husband, Jay Tidmarsh, have been married twelve years and have three sons, Christopher, David, and Kevin.

MICHAEL BARKASY, from West Chester, Pennsylvania, is in his senior year at Notre Dame. He is majoring in science-preprofessional Studies and History, and continues to visit the house of a senior citizen after his course in Theology and Community Service. He plans to attend medical school after graduation.

KATIE BERGIN is a volunteer with the Holy Cross Associates Program in Pocurro, Chile. Katie graduated from Notre Dame in 1994 with a degree in the Program for liberal studies and theology and participated in programs with both the Center for Social Concerns and Campus Ministry.

ROBERT ELMER is a 1994 graduate of Notre Dame in the Program for liberal studies, who was involved with many programs with the Center for Social Concerns and Campus Ministry. Bob is now at St. Francis Health Center in the Adolescent Treatment Center in Colorado Springs, Colorado, as a Holy Cross Associate.

SARAH KEYES is a 1994 graduate of Notre Dame with a degree in English. She participated at Notre Dame in service learning programs with the Center for Social Concerns and Campus Ministry. Presently, she is a Holy Cross Associate in Brockton, Massachusetts, working at St. Vincent's Home with troubled youth.

RONALD WHITE'S journey of faith and action began in a Southern Baptist church in Columbus, Georgia as a volunteer and picketer for SNCC, and continues now within the St. John's Catholic community in Columbia, Maryland and through his work for the Campaign for Human Development, the Bishops' anti-poverty campaign. Ron entered Catholic seminary at age fourteen and began giving talks on black power and integration to audiences in rural Wisconsin during his junior and senior years in high school. He left the seminary program in college and completed a B.A. in Philosophy at Dominican College in Racine, Wisconsin, while also taking part in student protests against the Vietnam War and becoming interested in the emerging feminist movement. In 1980, he received an M.A. in the History and Philosophy of Religions from Miami University in Ohio. After graduate school, he worked for the

Archdiocese of Milwaukee, exploring more effective methods of adult education, and eventually became director of the Justice and Peace office. In 1988, Ron was hired by the U.S. Catholic Conference where for the past five years he has been working with dioceses and low-income groups through the Campaign for Human Development. Ron and his wife Monica have two sons, Micah and Jamal.

RESOURCES FOR CONTINUING CONVERSATIONS

Books

Chapter 1   Gutierrez, Gustavo. *The God of Life*. Maryknoll: Orbis Books, 1991.

LaCugna, Catherine Mowry. *God for Us: The Trinity and Christian Life*. San Francisco: HarperCollins, 1991.

McFague, Sallie. *Models of God: Theology for an Ecological, Nuclear Age*. Philadelphia: Fortress Press, 1987.

Nouwen, Henri J.M. *The Return of the Prodigal Son*. New York: Doubleday, 1992.

Chapter 2   Dunne, John S. *The Reasons of the Heart.*. Notre Dame: Notre Dame Press, 1978.

Vanier, Jean. *Be Not Afraid*. Mahwah: Paulist Press, 1975.

Chapter 3   Nouwen, Henri J.M. *Out of Solitude*. Notre Dame: Ave Maria Press, 1978.

Vanier, Jean. *Community and Growth*. Mahwah: Paulist Press, 1989.

Chapter 4   Henriot, Peter. *Opting for the Poor*. Washington, D.C.: Center of Concern, 1990.

National Conference of Catholic Bishops. *Communities of Salt and Light*, 1993.

Nouwen, Henri. *Creative Ministry*. New York: Doubleday, 1991.

————. *Reaching Out*. New York: Doubleday, 1975.

————. *The Wounded Healer*. New York: Doubleday, 1990.

Nouwen, McNeill, Morrison. *Compassion: A Reflection on the Christian Life*. New York: Doubleday, 1983.

Chapter 5   Boff, Leonardo, and Virgilio Elizondo, eds. *1492–1992: The Voice of the Victims*. Philadelphia: Trinity Press International, 1990.

150

Nouwen, McNeill, Morrison. *Compassion. Op. cit.*
Ricoeur, Paul. *The Symbolism of Evil.* Boston: Beacon Press, 1967.

Chapter 6 Brown, Robert McAfee. *Unexpected News: Reading the Bible with Third-World Eyes.* London: Westminster Press, 1984.
Himes, Michael J. and Kenneth R. Himes. *Fullness of Faith: The Public Significance of Theology.* New York: Paulist Press, 1994.
Rupp, Joyce. *May I Have This Dance?* Notre Dame: Ave Maria Press, 1989.

Chapter 7 Cooke, Bernard. *Sacraments and Sacramentality.* Mystic: Twenty-Third, 1983.
Hellwig, Monika. *The Meaning of the Sacraments.* Dayton: Pflaum, 1972.
Lawler, Michael G. *Symbol and Sacrament: A Contemporary Sacramental Theologian.* New York: Paulist Press, 1987.
Osborne, Kenan B. *Sacramental Theology: A General Introduction.* New York: Paulist Press, 1988.

Chapter 8 Léon-Dufour, Xavier. *Sharing the Eucharistic Bread: The Witness of the New Testament.* New York: Paulist Press, 1987.
Nouwen, Henri J.M. *With Burning Hearts: A Meditation on the Eucharistic Life.* Maryknoll: Orbis Books, 1994.
Ruether, Rosemary Radford. *Women-Church: Theology and Practice of Feminist Liturgical Communities.* San Francisco: Harper & Row, 1985.

Chapter 9 Day, Dorothy. *The Long Loneliness.* Chicago: Thomas More Press, 1989.
Dunne, John S. *The Way of All the Earth.* Notre Dame: Notre Dame Press, 1978.
Fischer, Kathleen R. *The Inner Rainbow: The Imagination in Christian Life.* New York: Paulist Press, 1983.
Merton, Thomas. *The Courage for Truth.* New York: Farrar, Straus, Giroux, 1993.

Videos

Himes, Michael. "The Mystery of Faith: An Introduction to Catholicism with Father Michael Himes." A series of ten videos with extensive study guide, available from Corpus Video Inc., Box 727, Jefferson Valley, NY 10535-9910, or call 1-800-795-0444. The titles are: Grace, Salvation, Church Tradition, Trinity, Incarnation, Sacraments of Vocation, Baptism, Reconciliation, and Eucharist. These videos are also available directly from Paulist Press, 201-825-7300.

Michael Himes and collaborators at meeting at the C.S.C. at Notre Dame